# SPIKEY

# *2 Hard to Handle*

The Autobiography of Mike 'Spikey' Watkins

With Anthony Bunko

## St David's Press

Cardiff

Published in Wales by St. David's Press, an imprint of

Ashley Drake Publishing Ltd
PO Box 733
Cardiff
CF14 7ZY

www.st-davids-press.com

First Impression – 2014

ISBN
978-1-902719-40-5

© Ashley Drake Publishing Ltd 2014
Text © Mike Watkins & Anthony Bunko 2014

British Library Cataloguing-in-Publication Data.
A CIP catalogue for this book is available from the British Library.

Typeset by Replika Press Pvt Ltd, India
Cover designed by www.cr-eative.co.uk
Printed by CPI Group (UK) Ltd

# Contents

*To my five wonderful Grandsons*
*(Josh, Sam, Jack Dare, Luke and Oscar)*
*But don't forget...none of you are allowed*
*to read this until you are 21!*

# Acknowledgements

I would like to thank all my friends in Molly Malone's (Trevor Allen, Jason Dinsdale, Gareth Hughes, Tim Richardson, Huw Carey, Brian Doyle, Irish Diamond John Campbell, BB and Michael) for making this book possible. If they hadn't pushed me into it, I would never have had my life story put in print. Also all the gang from The Cross Keys Hotel back in Wales (Darren Parry and his son Coel, Roy, Derek and Longie) for persuading me to do it.

My two wonderful daughters for loving me. My son-in-law Gareth Chubb of C-reative Design in Cardiff for doing the book cover and helping me with a load of other stuff.

All those people who have given up their time to help me recall stories and have given me quotes. A special thanks to Paul Turner for writing the Foreword and for being such a good friend and a great player.

Of course, I must mention the larger-than-life Charlie Faulkner. What would I have done without him? We had a ball over the years, both on and off the rugby field. Also Roy Duggan who was the backs coach with us at Newport, and for all those others players who I haven't got around to mentioning and the clubs who became a massive part of my life.

Others I would like to mention are, John Kealy, Row, Christof and the rest of the gang from the Dubliner pub in Bangkok for many, many lost nights of Celtic celebrations. Also a massive thanks to Gareth Hughes, the Managing Director of the RSM Thailand Accountant and Legal Firm and all of his wonderful staff.

Special thanks to Anthony Bunko, who worked so hard in putting my ramblings into some kind of order and keeping me focused. We are now friends for life (and again Huw Carey for introducing me to Anthony...the Merthyr Connection). Also Ashley Drake for being brave enough to take the book on through his publishing company, St. David's Press.

Finally of course, my darling Maew, and her children, who have shown me how to be a better human being.

**Spikey**
**Bangkok**
**February 2014**

# Preface

Mike 'Spikey' Watkins is one of the most charismatic & personable characters it has been my undoubted privilege to have ever met. A man's man & their undoubted leader, at another time and a different place his call to 'fix bayonets' would have received instant compliance, for wherever he intended sending you, he had been himself and was determined to go again.

No history of Welsh Rugby in the 1970s & '80s would be complete without his presence in it. Shunned as a pariah by the rugby establishment for large parts of his playing career, amongst the rugby public and his fellow players he was revered as one of Welsh rugby's great characters. Tough as teak, he might kick all your teeth in and break your arm for mumbling but he could play rugby too and when it was all over, he was not only sure to make you laugh but convince you that it was all your fault in the first place anyway. His was the first name that you looked for on the opposition roster and the one you wanted most on your own side.

If there is a heaven, my version of it is a seat on the Crawshays tour bus as it tumbles through the endless French countryside, one fight behind us and many more ahead. Glenn Webbe is performing courtesy of the Magic Circle and Spikey is compering events from a mic at the front of the bus. As I reflect on what heaven and happiness really is, I hope that the Good Lord will amble down the aisle and ask me what I think. I shall look at him in all his glory & say, 'I think, I think Lord, that you're bloody lucky to be on Spikey's bus.

**Chris Callaghan**
**Cambridge, Aberavon and Bridgend.**

# Foreword

When I was a kid of about nine or ten, most Saturday afternoons us boys used to go across to Abercarn Welfare to watch the local soccer team, Abercarn Rangers. On the field above at the same time, there was often a game of rugby taking place, usually involving local, junior side Cwmcarn Youth.

As sure as eggs are eggs within twenty minutes someone would shout out, 'It's all kicked off on the top field', at which all us youngsters would run as a group to see the fighting taking place. Usually after the very stressed-out officials had separated the brawlers and the commotion had died down, all we'd hear was, "It was that Watkins boy again"

For us young Valley boys were always looking for a local hero. Someone we could follow, not necessarily emulate in typical 'Spikey' fashion but to follow the challenge and his bravery. His notoriety made him every bit a hero for us youngsters, certainly in our part of Monmouthshire.

Little did I know that I'd play in the same side as 'that Watkins boy' years later and we'd become such great friends on and off the field. What I loved about him was there was always a method somewhere within that madness of his and he's been great company over the years!!

At 17 I followed Spikey's path to Crumlin RFC which was about a mile from my home in Newbridge. It was there that he had played before joining Cardiff.

Crumlin village, with its famous viaduct, colliery and rugby club was a very good so-called 'second-class' club which played other local clubs like Bedwas, Abercarn, Pontypool Utd,

Blaenavon, Risca, Cwmbran, Blackwood, and Talywain in what were hugely competitive times. It was a great introduction into rugby and it definitely taught players how to survive and grow up, both as a man and a rugby player. It proved to be a very fertile breeding ground for unearthing many players and stars that went on to play in the more famous elite first class system.

Stories of Spike's notoriety on and off the field were evident every time I walked into Crumlin Rugby Club. The club house trophy cabinet was stacked full of the many jerseys presented to the club by Mike from his days at Cardiff after playing against lots of touring sides. What was missing at the time was the more coveted Welsh jersey and cap, but that would come in time.

During my two enjoyable years at Crumlin we were drawn against Cardiff in the WRU Schweppes Cup at Cardiff Arms Park. Nowadays the result would be a cricket score, and the Cardiff club side these days are not a patch on the side we met before Christmas in the 1978/79 season. Just to remind everyone, Cardiff had a side at the time containing the likes of Gareth Davies, Terry Holmes, Barry Nelmes, Alan Phillips, Alex Finlayson, Chris Camilleri, Stuart Lane, John Scott, Robert Norster, Hans de Goede, Mike Knill and many others. All ready to destroy little old Crumlin. I remember it clearly as it was the week before the more famous Wales v NZ 'Andy Haden diving incident' game.

On the day, we played out of our skins and arrived at half time at the Arms Park with the score 0-0. We finally succumbed to a two-try defeat, 12-0, which was nearly as good as a win for us.

Cardiff players and committee were full of praise for our efforts, but what they didn't know was that their hooker Spikey had helped us the week before. As he'd been banned by the

WRU and Cardiff themselves for the famous nightclub incident, he'd told us all about their calls and tap penalty moves. We had played well, but Spike had certainly played his part.

A few years later, tales of his leadership qualities tempted me to follow him down the Valley to Newport during the 85/86 season. I grew up admiring the big 'Town' side but was raised typically within my Valley community to despise the townies who had always been accused of stealing the best players from our village sides up the Valleys. This didn't go down too well with all the Valley clubs throughout those years.

I'm not really sure why or how Spikey joined Newport. Even though we enjoyed a couple of great seasons there, I never really thought of him as a 'Newport' player. To me he was always a Cwmcarn Youth, Crumlin and Cardiff player. I think he joined because of his friendship with Tony 'Charlie' Faulkner, the coach at the time. He had been in the Welsh squad together with Charlie and had a great amount of respect him as a player.

"Charlie's and Spikey's Newport," went from a poor side nearly bottom of the Championship to one of the best teams in the league in a very short time. I joined because they had put together a juggernaut pack of forwards that could challenge the likes of Cardiff, Llanelli, Neath and Pontypool. It was a pleasure to play behind them.

That Spike was never given any credit for this should still embarrass some people then involved in the Newport Club. During that era the club jumped from bottom of the league table to near the top, breaking try and point-scoring records. But this remains overlooked due to petty and childish attitudes from the people in charge.

Michael John Watkins captained his country from that club, but if you walk into the Rodney Parade clubhouse, lining their walls are 'The Captains of Wales', photos of players who have captained their country while playing for Newport. Yet there is no photograph of M.J. Watkins. An unbelievably poor show!! People, and they know exactly who they are, should hang their heads in shame!

To sum up, simply, Michael John Watkins was not only a great friend to me while growing up but also a great inspiration to me and all the teams he has played for and coached. Going into battle you could always rely on him when the muck and bullets started. Even though he probably started it!!

**Paul Turner**
**February 2014**

# 1

# Hookers Night Out

*"Not afraid of anything or anyone he also had great skills. The perfect hooker. I believe if he had been managed the right way he could have been one of the greatest hookers ever to have played the game."*

**Phil Kingsley Jones**
**Coach - Manager - Administrator - Entertainer**

Cardiff Arms Park, March 17<sup>th</sup>, 1979. A bitterly cold and overcast Saturday afternoon. The atmosphere in the stadium bordered on hysteria. Forty-six thousand, fanatical, and mostly drunk, Welshmen singing their hearts out. Enough passion in their gravelled voices to fuel a 10-ton steam train to Bangor and back.

Every schoolboy's dream. No, not just every schoolboy's, every Welshman's, dream. To pull on that red shirt and stand toe to toe against the old enemy. The English; the Red Rose; the White Juggernaut. Them lot of posh bastards from over the bridge.

'How do you feel Spikey?' Gerry Wallace, a good friend and fellow player at Cardiff Rugby Club, looked me straight in the eyes.

'How do you think I feel?' I replied, 'bloody awful.'

From my seat in the West Stand I watched with envy as both teams lined up on the halfway line ready for the National Anthems.

'Well you should feel awful. If you hadn't been so stupid, it would be you down there now, not him' He pointed to where Alan Phillips stood on the field, his chest puffed out with pride. On his back, the number two shirt. My number two shirt.

Like a moody teenager, I shrugged and slumped lower into my seat. God only knows why the hell I'd let Gerry talk me into coming to watch the game in the first place. I'd never been a great watcher of sport. It's a bit like having sex. Great if you are doing it yourself, not so clever watching someone else getting their rocks off, unless you are into that sort of thing and I definitely wasn't. So to be sitting there, all alone, amongst a cast of thousands, looking at my most bitter rival running around the hallowed turf instead of me was like rolling all of my worst fears up into one big nightmare.

I imagined every person in the famous old stadium glaring across at me. All of them nudging each other and sniggering under their breath. It made me feel like the 'baddie' strolling out on stage in some kind of pantomime. A pantomime organised and directed, but not bloody funded of course, by the Welsh Rugby Union.

'Who are you lot staring at?' I would cry out, a long black cloak partially covering my features.

'You...you idiot,' they would all yell back. 'Look what you've done this time.' Their imaginary verbal abuse prodding me from all directions.

'But it wasn't my fault,' I'd protest.

'Oh yes it was.'

'Oh no it wasn't.'

'Oh yes it was.'

'Oh no it......oh...shut up and watch the bloody match,' I'd mutter and slump down even further.

As the last strains of Hen Wlad Fy Nhadau echoed around the ground, my mind drifted back to that November night a few months earlier. An innocent Thursday which subsequently ended up costing me my first and at that time, only chance of winning a Welsh international rugby cap.

'Fancy a quick beer,' I asked Jeff Davies as we got changed next to each other. We had just finished our final training session in Cardiff before the B international against France the coming Saturday in Aberavon. It had been a long wait for me. After what seemed like an eternity, I had again been selected to start a B international, and Jeff, the Bridgend hooker, got picked on the bench. I was more than ready. I'd trained hard for it, and more importantly, I'd kept my nose clean for a change.

Hang on, hang on now, I can hear you all muttering as you read this, *'what was he doing, going for a beer two days before an international rugby match?'* Let me explain. First off, it was my way of building a bond with Jeff. We had been fierce rivals over the years and when we played against each other normally, neither of us took a step backwards. In my simple way of thinking, we were now both on the same side, so chilling out and having a brew would be a good way to get to know each other instead of us both trying to punch one another's heads clean off.

Secondly, rugby wasn't a professional sport in those days. I wasn't earning a living from playing the game I loved and I didn't have to answer to anyone, so if I fancied a drink I could have one. The WRU wasn't my boss, even if their committees acted as though they thought they were. They didn't pay me a wage. I drove a truck for twelve hours a day to do that. Plus in those days, rugby players the world over weren't teetotal gym monkeys like most of them are today. We were simple folk. We did simple things...well. We trained hard, we drunk hard, we played hard, and we drunk even harder after the game. Ok, there may have been a bit of shagging and eating curry mixed in there somewhere, but I didn't want to bore you with all that detail...not just yet! Bruised and battered on a Sunday morning, it was back up the club to top ourselves up from the night before. Then first thing Monday morning, it was off to work to earn money for the family, not having a relaxing morning massage in some sports complex.

On that fateful Thursday night, showered and shaved, Jeff and I headed off for a few jars in the centre of Cardiff. After a bit of a wander we ended up in Qui Qui's wine bar in Charles Street. As usual the place was bouncing with wall-to-wall talent. Girls of every shape and size strutting their stuff on the dance floor. One beer led to two. Two beers led to three, three led to...well you get the picture.

Giving it a bit of the old Valleys charm, I started fooling about with some girls dancing near us. Nothing too serious mind, just a laugh and a mess about but, and I don't know how, a glass or two got accidentally smashed. A couple of bouncers rushed over looking for trouble. Jeff and I stood our ground, two hookers in arms.

They told us to leave. I refused. We hadn't done anything wrong. Ok, looking back now, maybe I should have left, backed down and walked away, especially with my big game coming up. But rightly or wrongly, walking away or backing down has never been in my nature. If someone asked me to do something that I didn't want to do, I wouldn't do it. If I was told to do something, and even if I really wanted to do it, I normally went out of my way to do the complete and utter opposite. So a few bouncers in monkey suits, telling me to get out was just like waving a big red rag to a stocky, no-nonsense, Abercarn bull.

By then, the red mist had well and truly descended. Wild horses pulling chains wrapped around my ankles wouldn't have dragged me out of there.

'I'm not going anywhere,' I stared at them.

After a bit of eyeballing, a little pushing and shoving, the bouncers retreated.

'Yes!' victory was ours. Or so I thought.

The next thing I knew, the Old Bill had arrived in force. We were informed that if we didn't leave we would be spending the night in the cells. One copper in particular took great pride laying down the heavy arm of the law. He started pushing me out towards the exit. Then I remembered my sheepskin coat in the cloak room. To be honest, I should have left the bloody thing there. It made me look like Del Boy from Fools and Horses.

'Oh! Hang on. My coat.' I shouted as I tried to break free to go and get it.

The same copper grabbed my collar, real aggressive like and pushed me into the door.

'Oh! I've got to get my coat.' I struggled, 'That coat cost me a couple of bob,' I yelled, but he wouldn't listen to a word of it. He kept tugging me. Unwisely, I gave him a bit of a push back. Nothing heavy, I wasn't that stupid. However, that was the excuse he had been looking for. A few choice words later, Jeff and I got thrown into the back of the waiting Black Maria. It sped off through the streets of Cardiff, lights flashing, sirens wailing, the Full bloody Monty.

They manhandled us out of the van and into the station. On seeing me, the sergeant on duty behind the counter, smiled. 'How's it going Spikey? What the hell's going on?' Apparently, he was a massive Cardiff rugby supporter.

'Well I was doing alright until this bloody....' I stopped short of calling the arresting officer a few more choice names.

'Go stand over there for a minute, Spike. I'll see if I can sort it out,' the sergeant whispered to me.

From across the room, I could hear them arguing. The sergeant strolled back shaking his head. 'Sorry Spike, looks like you are going in the book.'

The arresting officers looked very pleased with their night's work.

'Just wanting to make a name for yourself, are you, you prat?' I spat my words at one of the coppers. His smirk grew wider.

They charged us both with being drunk and disorderly and banged us up for the night. To this day, I still don't think we did anything really wrong. I certainly wasn't drunk. We had been messing about, but again I didn't think we had been disorderly.

In the end I knew it would come down to the copper's word against mine. I was a short, stocky, rugby player from the Valleys; he was a lanky prat in a uniform from Cardiff. What chance did I have? The next morning, Jeff and I agreed to plead guilty. In my mind, the sooner we got it over with the better. I assumed we would just pay whatever fine they threw at us and, naively, that no one would be any the wiser.

Or so I thought. I was in for a big shock. Outside the police station that morning, several TV cameras and reporters surrounded us as we strolled out.

I couldn't understand how they knew we were there. I wondered who had informed the press we'd been locked up. I couldn't be sure, but I had a good idea!

The front page headlines in the local paper later that afternoon screamed out in large bold letters. 'Hookers Night Out!" followed by a photo of me and Jeff.

Of course, the bad news spread like wildfire. By the time I got home there was a telegram from the WRU waiting for me. It said, '*It has been brought to our attention....blah, blah, blah.*' At the end of the letter it simply stated, '*Your services are no longer required and you have been dropped from the game on Saturday.*'

Sitting in my front room, I read the last line of the letter over and over again.

'*Your services are no longer required.*'

'*Your services are no longer required.*'

*'Your services are no longer required.'*

The maddening thing was that no one from the WRU bothered to call to hear my side of the story. I'd simply got dropped from the side. Hung, drawn and quartered without so much as a word in my defence. We could have been completely innocent, for all they knew. Over the years I would discover, to my cost, that this was how the Welsh Rugby Union operated. To them, I was always guilty until proven even guiltier.

Alright, there had been a little smoke to go with the fire, but not enough to turn us into public enemies numbers one and two. To me it was a bit of larking about, a few words and that was that. No big deal! But to others, it became a massive deal.

In hindsight, maybe we shouldn't have pleaded guilty. If I had pleaded not guilty, perhaps I could have played on the Saturday and carried on playing up until the trial. But I honestly didn't think much would come of it.

To add to the shame and the injustice, Alan Phillips, who played at the same club as me, got drafted in to play the B international.

Worse was still to come. Cardiff, my own club, picked up on the situation and I got summoned to a meeting the week after. I walked the 'long green mile' into the committee room, where they sat in their crumpled blazers and food-stained ties, necking warm beer. Once again, I felt I was sentenced before I had the opportunity to open my mouth.

*Guilty as charged, your honour!*

I got banned from playing for Cardiff from December 1st until the end of the season. I'm sure Eric Cantona got less than me, and he Kung Fu-kicked someone in the crowd. All I did was get into a bit of bother in a nightclub with some bouncers.

Unlike Wales, Cardiff did let me carry on training with them. Well for a while, they did. Still angry, I would race about the field like an Exocet Missile on a one-way mission to hurt certain

7

individuals. After a few sessions they politely asked me not to bother training with them until my full ban had been served. I don't really blame them. Where my head was, I wouldn't have been happy until I'd done some serious damage.

Then, believe it or not, my luck went from bad, to worse, to terrible. In the 1979 Five Nations Championship, Bobby Windsor, who hadn't missed a single game when I had been on the bench for Wales for the five previous years, was unavailable for the last match. He had developed nasty skin burns while playing for Pontypool against Cardiff, after a groundsman lined the pitch with quicklime instead of chalk. His injury meant he was detained in hospital, and ruled him out of the big one, Wales versus England. What's more, if Wales won it meant another Triple Crown and the Championship.

To cut a long story short, Phillips, who hadn't had a look-in until my arrest in the November, got promoted into the proper Welsh side for the game in Cardiff. That was the only reason I was sat in the stands, feeling angry and despondent, instead of being down on the field.

When Gerry had called to ask me to go to the game and see Phillips get his first cap, I thought he was joking.

'No Gerry, that's the last thing I want to do.'

'I know it is,' he said, 'but that's why I want to take you down.'

I really didn't want to go. I couldn't even go into Cardiff's Athletic Club before the game for a drink, because I was banned from there as well. I didn't know what they thought I was going to do. Maybe assassinate Phillips with a bullet from the Grassy Knoll as he ran out on the field?

Wales won the match easily on the day, and to be fair although I hate to say it, Phillips played well.

In a funny way I was glad Gerry insisted on taking me to that match. It made me look at myself in the mirror and ask some fundamental questions. It may have been the worst day of my sporting life but it also proved a turning point for me. I sat there while the crowd cheered and clapped the boys off the field. I stared across at the section full of the WRU committeemen. There they stood, smiles on their smug faces, patting each other on the backs for a job well done. I stared long and hard at the one committeeman who had pulled me aside a few weeks before to tell me I would 'Never, ever play for Wales in a million years.' They regarded me as a rebel, a misfit and *"enfant terrible"* of Welsh rugby.

As I slowly walked out of the stadium, I muttered to myself, 'Right, you bunch of bastards, I'll bloody show you!'

# 2

# 50 Shades of Spikey!

*"Spikey Watkins, a lad from a small valley town who went on to become one of the most inspirational leaders that Welsh rugby has ever produced. His story is fascinating. The boy from the valleys makes good. The man the establishment ignored for so long finally gets his chance and delivers. I can identify with that!*

**Mike Ruddock**
**Blaina - Tredegar - Swansea - Wales Coach 2004-06**

From an early age, trouble followed me around like my wicked shadow. I wasn't a tearaway or a thug; let's just say I may have been considered a very 'active' child. Nothing proved too hot or too heavy for me. My Gran often said I had been at the front of the queue when God handed out daring and cunning. In the same breath, she added I must have been close to the back when it came to showing respect for anyone in authority!

As clever as clogs, my Gran.

I remember just turning nine years old, without a care in the world and definitely without any fear, scaling a five-foot wall. Balancing on the edge, I stared at the sharp metal railings standing between me and my goal, to pinch as many apples from a neighbour's garden as I could. The thing was, I didn't even want to eat them. They tasted too sour. It was just something to do. Something to break up the boredom.

Carefully, I began to inch my way over the railings. As usual my mate, Doc Cooper, was the lookout down below.

Half way over, both my feet slipped from under me. I toppled backwards and impaled myself on one of the spikes. The cold, rusty, metal railing ripped an 8 inch hole in my guts, just to the left of my belly button.

Doc laughed at first. Then he heard my screams and saw the blood. I'm not sure how, maybe in complete panic, I got myself off the railings. The pain was excruciating. Blood gushed everywhere. My tee-shirt and jeans were saturated. Even my shoes and socks were soaked through. I hobbled home as if shot by a sniper. A trail of blood followed me to my front door.

After the initial shock my mother took control of the situation, as she always did. My father, as usual, was away driving his truck. Gently, a couple of people placed me into the back of a neighbour's car. At the hospital, it was a mad panic. I got rushed straight through the waiting rooms and into the operating theatre. I woke up feeling groggy, lying in a hospital bed on the ward. My mother stood over me, a weak smile on her face.

By the time I'd healed up and gone back to school, sporting a horrendous looking scar, my name in the yard had unsurprisingly changed from Mike, to Spike, before resting, rather comfortably, at the front door of...Spikey. And that's where's it's stayed ever since. A painful but memorable way of earning a nickname, I guess. On saying that, it could have been worse. I could have tripped over the lino in the kitchen and impaled myself on a frying pan! Mike 'Frying Pan' Watkins wouldn't have been a name I would have been proud of.

I got little sympathy off my old man on his return home. If the truth be known, he didn't do sympathy, or compliments or encouragement either. Traits I got used to down the years. He was a hard man in every sense of the word. Extremely hard working but also as hard as nails, especially as far as I was concerned. Maybe it had something to do with his upbringing or maybe his time in the army. I really don't know.

Born in Usk in 1919, my father, Arthur John Watkins came from a reasonably successful family. My father's father, who I never met, was a haulage contractor from the Forest of Dean. He supplied the pits throughout Wales with wooden props, which before the introduction of motorized vehicles were transported by horses.

With little formal education, my father unsurprisingly left school to go and work in the family business until World War II came along. He spent most of his army life with the South Wales Borderers fighting out in Burma against the Japanese. He reached the rank of Regimental Sergeant Major and returned home a hero after receiving the Military Medal for bravery after saving Captain Bryn Smith's life. From what I can gather, he became something of a local hero with his photograph splashed over the papers. He also received life membership to many of the local clubs. Yet, he rarely talked about his time in the war. He kept his medals locked away in a bureau in his bedroom.

He met my mother, Kitty Thomas, at a local tea-dance when the war was over. A very attractive looking girl, she held the glamorous title of Miss Carnival Queen. Yet she was the one who once told me she had fancied my father the first time she set eyes on him because, in her words, 'he looked like a bit of rough.' My father, not usually known for his jovial wit, did actually joke to me on that occasion that from what he remembered it was the other way around.

Whilst he was quite a serious individual, my mother happened to be the complete opposite. Always laughing and joking. A typical Valleys girl with a great sense of humour coated with a heart of gold. One of her favourite sayings when I said something stupid was, 'Michael, I'll put your head in a plastic bag to keep it fresh.'

Like most of the men in the area, my mother's father worked in the local colliery. Sadly he also died before I ever met him. From an early age, my mother's mother, Maud Thomas had been sent away to work in service for a wealthier family. Not unusual for a young Welsh girl from a family with little money or opportunity.

She was a great old girl, my Gran. I spent more time with her than anyone else in my family. Being the only boy, unceremoniously dumped in the middle of a gaggle of three girls, I often stayed with her just to get away from all the shrieking and squawking in my house.

My sister Jayne was already four years old when I arrived, kicking and screaming on the 9th January 1952. The doctors took one look at me and told my mother she couldn't have any more babies. I imagine them thinking, *"Bloody hell, we can't allow too many more nutters like this into the world."* My mother never accepted it. A fortune teller told her she would definitely have more children, and that's what she believed. Then, Abracadabra, four years later, I ended up with twin sisters, Susan and Elizabeth.

My mother loved all that psychic mumbo-jumbo. When I was very, very young, a clairvoyant reading her tea-bags, or tea-leaves, or whatever they do, told her, her daughter would waltz through life and do really well. In later years, Jayne became a successful business woman, working for British Telecom as a personnel director. When it came to me, the fortune-teller didn't seem too confident of my 'waltzing through life' capabilities.

'Michael will find life a lot tougher,' she hesitated when telling my mother, 'but I can see him one day wearing red and running out on a field in front of many, many people and they will all applaud him.'

My mother took this as a sign. A sign I would definitely be the first Welsh bullfighter. No, only joking. She was convinced I would one day play rugby for Wales. 'It is your destiny,' she often told me, 'it's been written in the tea-bags!'

Even during the darkest period of my rugby career, when I kept getting banned, she never once stopped believing. Everyone else, including me, did. It got to the point, where I thought I'd have more chance of actually becoming a bloody bullfighter than playing rugby for Wales.

I would say, 'Mam, it ain't going to happen.'

She'd reach across and grab my arm. 'Michael, the fortune teller told me you would. So you will.'

Up to the age of around four, we lived in a two-up, two-down house at Number 1 Canal Terrace, on the banks of the canal in Abercarn. I can only recall two things about that time. One was my father falling into the canal after staggering across the lock one evening, drunk. The other was the rats. The size of collie dogs, they were. Seemed like hundreds of them, scurrying all over the place. I hated them!

Leaving the rodent-infested house by the canal behind, we moved to a nice, modern house in the middle of a large green field. 87 High Meadow in Abercarn would have been just perfect if it wasn't for the thousands of other council houses someone decided to build around it.

With a population of less than 5000, Abercarn was one of those typical Gren cartoon-style villages. A grey and damp Welsh mining town located ten miles from Newport, with its rows and rows of terraced houses balanced on the side of the mountain. A rugby pitch located on a slope next to a river and of course, the obligatory coal mine blotting out the landscape.

The coal mine at Abercarn not only brought work to the area, it also brought large amounts of tragedy and sadness. My Gran often told me the story of the worst disaster which occurred there, on 11th September in 1878, when 238 local miners, men and boys, six of whom were just 13, lost their lives in the most bizarre and tragic of circumstances. An underground explosion, probably caused by a safety lamp, ripped through the Prince of Wales Colliery. The smoke and heat from the fire at the pit bottom made any rescue attempt almost impossible. With miners still missing, the manager of the site made a decision to flood the mine. Over 30 million gallons of water was piped down the shaft to put the fire out. In total it took eight weeks to extinguish the blaze. Apparently, the manager who flooded the mine topped himself years later.

Heartbreaking stuff!

Being warned never to play around the colliery by my parents only made me want to play there even more and, looking back, it was a stupid thing to do. The entire place was a death trap. But a death trap that was only a stone's throw away from my house and much too great a temptation to resist. It became my very own Barry Island Adventure Playground. Never mind rides like the Log Flume and The Ghost Ride. Ours were a lot more exciting and dangerous than all the scariest rides put together.

How my mates and I didn't get killed, I still don't know.

One of the craziest things we did was riding the empty coal buckets. We would climb up the electrical pylon, and that wasn't even the dangerous part, and then as the empty buckets passed, we leapt in and held on for dear life. It felt like I was riding the chairlifts in a French ski resort. We'd stay on right up until the last minute, then jump off, just before the buckets disappeared back into the mouth of the pit.

The miners kept chasing us away. But we didn't fear danger; we were indestructible. Well, that was until one of my mates had his middle finger pulled out when he didn't jump off the buckets in time. I suggested calling him, Billy Three Fingers and One Thumb after that. He wasn't amused.

'You were a complete bloody nightmare,' one of my sisters commented, when I asked her to describe what I was like to grow up with. She reminded me of the day I stripped the wheels off the twin's new toy prams to make myself a wooden go-cart.

'I needed a go-cart,' I reminded her.

'And what about the bats?' she hit back.

I still don't think that was my fault. It wasn't me who let the bats escape. She did! Ok, I was the one who found the bats up on the mountain in the first place and hid them in my 'castle' bedroom. And I wasn't the one who opened the bedroom door while the creatures were happily flying around inside. Unfortunately, she did. It ended up like a scene from a bad British vampire movie. Scared, flapping bats and screaming girls raced about the house.

I just needed something to keep me entertained all the time. Unlike kids of today, with their computers, and fancy phones and TV's in their bedroom, I had to make my own fun. One hot summer day, John Baker and I went looking for some rabbits up on the mountainside. We hunted and searched for ages but couldn't find any.

I had an idea. 'Let's burn them out of their holes,' I said.

With a box of stolen matches I lit the dry grass. We waited. The fire was slow to get going but when it did, there was no stopping it. Within minutes, half the mountain was ablaze. Smoke bellowed out down the Valley. We tried our best to put it out but to no avail. Sheep and other wildlife ran for their lives, followed closely by me and John!

On hearing the Fire Brigade in the distance, we kept our heads down behind some garages until everything cooled down a little. When I got home later, I must have looked a right sight. My eyes were all red and bloodshot, and I must have smelt like I'd smoked 20 Embassy Regal in one sitting.

From his chair, my father glanced up at me. 'Where have you been son?'

'Nowhere Dad...just out and about.'

I could feel his eyes piercing through my skin. 'You set the mountain on fire, didn't you?'

'No Dad I didn't, honest.' He rubbed his chin. I quickly added, 'I didn't Dad. I haven't been anywhere near the mountain.'

I knew, he knew, I did it. He let it drop, so thinking I was safe, I began to head towards my bedroombut he piped-up, 'Look, I know you did it. There were four of you, wasn't there?'

'No Dad, there was only me and John Baker.' I replied instantly.

He'd done up me like a kipper. He gave me a clip and locked me in my bedroom. That proved fruitless, because I got bored and stripped all the paper off the walls. He hit me again.

He tried his utmost to be strict with me. The problem was that for long periods of time he wasn't around to keep me under control. As his business went from strength to strength, we didn't see a lot of him. He won a contract to transport all kinds of stuff from the Tin Works to the docks in Newport and Liverpool and such like. It must have been really tough for my mother being the wife of a long-distance lorry driver while bringing up three girls and a hyperactive, stunt-boy, who had designs on being Batman, Superman and Evel Knievel all rolled up into one.

Later on, my old man got some work closer to home and for a while family life got a bit more stable. For better or worse, we saw a lot more of him. When I was about nine, he surprised me by giving me a brand new donkey jacket.

He must have picked it up from somewhere on his travels or won it in a bet as he'd never bought me anything. Yet, although it was a few sizes too big, I was chuffed to bits. Then at 4am the next morning, I discovered the real reason he'd got me the present. As I lay in bed fast asleep, he tapped me on the head. 'Come on son, get up.

'What? Where we going Dad?'

'Out.'

'Where?'

'An important job...hurry. Better put your new jacket on.'

I scrambled out of bed. Even though it was the middle of the night, I was excited to be going with my father. Then I found out why. For the next few hours, dressed in my nice, new, warm coat, he had me sneaking around the colliery, siphoning diesel out of the lorries. I should have known there would be a catch. We did this over and over again, night after night. Each morning I went to school, knackered, and smelling like a bloody petrol station. I hated that donkey jacket.

On saying that, I hated school just as much. Even at West End Junior School in Abercarn, I didn't want to go because the teachers hit me around the legs and hands with rulers. They probably wouldn't get away with behaviour like that today. One time my mother stormed down the school and had a blazing row with the teachers. It didn't do any good. They kept doing it.

After primary school, reluctantly, I headed to Cwmcarn Secondary Modern. I may as well have been sentenced to a four-year stretch in Borstal. Academically, I didn't have a clue what I wanted to be. I didn't dream of being an astronaut or a policeman or going to university. I just couldn't wait to get out of there. Maybe if their teaching style had been different, I may have done something else in my life, but I hated sitting behind a desk being talked at for eight hours a day. I felt so trapped.

Not having much of an education himself, my father really didn't care if I went to school or not. Knowing him, he probably left when he was in primary school to go and drive trucks!!

Frequently he'd let me bunk off lessons to go with him on the trucks. He didn't mind that at all. I think he saw it as an early apprenticeship for me to start to learn the ropes and keep the family haulage business going. Although it was boring as hell at times, it was still miles better than sitting in the classroom learning about Shakespeare and the like.

But then things got kind of strange. More often than not, he'd leave me in the cab and disappear for ages. I'm sure he was knocking someone off or going for a quick beer. One afternoon, we were out delivering coal in the back lanes around the area. He'd been gone whilst I sat in the cab listening to the radio. Then the cab door opened, 'Come on, get out,' he demanded.

I jumped down. 'Where are we going?'

'I want you to fight someone,' he muttered.

'What? Who?'

'Just some boy.'

'Why?'

He didn't reply. We turned the corner in one of the narrow back lanes. There stood a gang of kids. The biggest boy stood at the front rolling his shirt sleeves up. My Dad took my coat off me and whispered, 'Go on son, fight him.'

I didn't know what was happening or why I was doing it. I assumed the boy had done or said something to upset my Dad. The bigger boy ran at me and pushed me up against the wall. He rained punches into my body. Still confused, I covered up. In the background, I heard my father yelling out my namename, and as I didn't want to let him down I ended up battering the boy. In fact I almost beat him unconscious. In the end my Dad dragged me off him, my hands covered in blood.

As we walked away he just handed me my coat. He didn't say a word. It was odd. I never asked him why he wanted me to fight him. All these years later, I'm still uncertain why he made me do it. Perhaps, he thought I needed toughening up for all the challenges that lay ahead in my life. I really don't know.

I finally stopped going out with him. It got so weird, I went to school instead. When I did drag myself through the school gates I always seemed to be late. At least my excuses made the teachers laugh. 'My Nan died' or 'the rabbits got out and I had to find them before the dogs ate them', were the ones I used on a regular basis.

I arrived particularly late one morning and blurted out, 'Sorry sir, I had to help my Nan round up her rabbits.'

'I thought your Nan got buried last week.'

Quick as a flash I replied, 'My other Nan, Sir.'

Mrs Howells, my form teacher, wasn't really cut out to teach in such a hostile environment. She struggled to control her emotions, never mind our class. Often she'd take me to one side and say, 'Mike, can you try and keep them quiet please? I'll give you some chocolate if you can.'

'Hang on, Miss, you're the teacher.'

'Yeah, but they'll listen to you,' she added, 'you're a born leader.'

It was strange to hear her say that. I'd never thought of myself in that role. They say leaders are born but I'm not sure about that. Nevertheless she must have seen something in me because later in life I went on to lead nearly every team I ever played for.

Yet, up to that point, sport had never really been of interest to me. When playing football in the schoolyard as a young boy, I usually got picked last or put in goals. I didn't care. As long as I was making kids laugh I was more than happy.

Slowly that began to change.

After school I used to go along to Newbridge Youth Club. Next door was the famous Newbridge Boxing Club, which was renowned for being the gym where ex-World champion boxer Joe Calzaghe trained. I began messing about in there. I loved punching the bag and getting into the ring to have a dust up with someone.

I didn't play rugby until I was twelve. Not a bad thing in my book. Nowadays, kids playing full contact rugby when they're five and six is just plain crazy. By the time they reach their teens they are bored stiff with it all. In my opinion, kids should just play football or table tennis and other sports where they can hone their ball skills and more importantly, just enjoy it. Hopefully, I'm wrong, but the way it is going, in years to come, we'll have eight year-olds in the gym doing weights and bench presses. Utter nonsense. They should be out, climbing trees and enjoying life. Alright, maybe not riding buckets in the colliery or burning mountains down, but you know what I mean. Kids should be kids until they find the sport they like, not the other way around.

Mister Brian Hugget, a real disciplinarian, but fair, sports master at Cwmcarn gave me my first taste of rugby. From the off, he played me at hooker. I did double up as prop now and again, but hooker proved to be my position. Maybe it was my physique, or the fact I wasn't afraid to stick my head in where it hurt. Most likely, it was because he knew I wanted to have the ball as much as possible.

Quickly I progressed to play for the school team. Of course my mother was chuffed. In her mind, the prediction of the fortune teller and her PG Tips came one step closer. On the other hand, my father showed no interest whatsoever in any sport, never mind showing interest in his own son playing rugby.

But suddenly I had found my road to Damascus. Rugby gave me a focus. Even the other school teachers encouraged me. They proved to be a bunch of crafty bastards mind you. They used my newfound love of sport to keep me on the straight and narrow. They would warn me that if I didn't behave in their lessons, I wouldn't be allowed to play rugby for the school.

'Yes Sir, No Sir, Three bags full of crap sir.' I tried to curb my behaviour because I wanted to play rugby on a Saturday morning so much.

The first big, live, rugby match I remember going to see was when Llanelli came up to Cross Keys for a mid-week game under lights. It felt so exciting; the banter in the crowd; the sound of every tackle being made. A massive fist fight broke out, which excited me even more. Players like Delme Thomas and Norman Gale seemed to be like huge giants racing about the field.

I started following Newbridge and went to see them whenever possible. We never paid to get in, mind you. With my extensive knowledge of the colliery, my mates and I always sneaked in through the pit. Once there we'd shimmy across the gas pipe over the River Ebbw and into the ground. Occasionally if the pipe was too slippery, we watched from the top of the stock pile of coal. Sometimes we would end up dirtier than the players on the pitch.

I never got to see Wales play at the Arms Park in those days. Like I said, my old man was too busy working to be bothered with minor things like sport. I only saw them play on the TV. After the game we'd all be out on the field with a ball. Being kids, we'd all pretend to be our favourite players. Everyone wanted to be Welsh players but from the first moment I saw him. I wanted to be Alain Paco, the French hooker. He reminded me of a dog with a bone, and no one, no matter how big they were, was going to get it off him.

Pretty soon I got made captain of the school team and was later selected to play for Monmouthshire schools. At school boy level, however, that was as far as I got.

Years later, when I won my Welsh cap and captained my country, my daughters were still attending Cwmcarn Secondary school. I told my oldest to ask the teachers if they wanted me to present them with a Welsh jersey or a cap or even a photo of me captaining the team. I was really proud to be the only guy from the school to have achieved that feat.

Strangely enough, they never came back. Maybe they thought I was like some kind of evil, Count Dracula, who if invited back in through the school gates, would return to cause havoc in the corridors once again. I'm sure when I drove past recently they had a string of garlic, a big cross, and a sign saying, "Spikey keep out!" attached to the gate.

The funny thing is, today there are two schools in Bangkok with photos of me playing for Wales up on their walls. And they haven't really got a clue what rugby is. Now that is strange.

# 3

# Blood, Sweat and Stud Marks

*"What a player to have on your side. Spike was one of the fittest, if not the fittest. His strength in scrums and mauls was outstanding. Pre-season training was a run up Trinant coal tip. Spike sometimes arrived late from work when most of the players were already halfway up the tip. By the time they reached the top, Spike had passed them. He always wanted to be first!*

*It was a privilege for myself and other players to play with Spike at Crumlin Rugby Football Club."*

**Jeff Thomas**
**Crumlin RFC**

I first set eyes on Stephanie (my wife to be) when we were still both in school. I sat day-dreaming in the woodwork class one afternoon, trying to whittle a boat out of half a tree trunk and staring, not so innocently, at the girls out in the yard playing netball in their school issue, navy blue knickers.

I loved those navy blue knickers. I hated bloody woodwork!

Out of all the girls there, I couldn't take my eyes off the blonde one with the long legs. By the time the lesson finished, lust had got the better of me and my attempt at a wooden boat ended up the same way as the Titanic, at the bottom of the rubbish bin.

One of my mates asked one of her mates, if Stephanie fancied meeting me at a dance in Cwmcarn Youth Club on the Friday night. There was a group playing called The Midnight City Soul Band. Stephanie agreed. For Dutch courage before the dance, I went with some of the other boys to the off-licence.

The date itself started off fine, but then as usual it all kicked off in the dancehall. Youngsters pissed-up on cheap cider fought like banshees. Within five minutes the entire place looked like a battle scene from World War Cwmcarn. Everyone got involved in the fighting, including me, and the band. The dance got abandoned and I ended up walking Steph home with a lump on the side of my head from a sneaky right hook.

It didn't put her off and she became my first proper girlfriend. It didn't take us long to lose our virginity. A few months later at a house party, we managed to nab one of the bedrooms. I would like to think I was absolutely amazing in the sack and it was the best night of her life. In truth, it was kind of messy, uncomfortable and didn't take very long at all. Like most excited boys doing it for the first time, it was all over before it really got started, especially for her.

But I did improve, the more I practiced!

With not a cat-in-hell's chance of gaining any qualifications, I left school at fifteen and, to earn my keep, I worked night-shifts in Abercarn Tin Works as a machine operator. The department was made up mostly of women. A right scary lot. Like a pack of foul-mouthed hyenas they could undress a man with their eyes from over 500 yards away.

After a while I got used to them, thanks to my thick skin. Pretty soon I became the informal shop steward and the entertainments secretary in the same breath. The trick was that we used to knock-out all our week's work between Monday and Thursday, which meant Friday night in the factory became cabaret night. All the machines would be turned off and a make-shift stage erected at the top end of the factory. It was just like being in a local social club. We even had bingo to start. The women used to bring in plates of food, and flagons of drink.

The shows became legendary. They became the Abercarn Tin Works' version of the X-Factor, but with a lot more talent and a lot more fun.

Outside work, I began playing rugby for Cwmcarn Youth. There were some good youth sides about at that time like Pontypool United, and of course, Cardiff and Newport. Yet, we not only matched them, we beat them on a regular basis. We had a very strong side, very committed with an excellent mixture of playing ability and a pinch of thuggery thrown in for good measure.

I soon became the mouthy captain. One of my favourite sayings at all levels during my rugby career was: 'If violence starts, I'd rather get sent off than carried off.' To me, there was no shame to walk off the field for an early bath after giving someone a shoeing. Being carried or helped off the field when someone gave you a clip was unthinkable.

My approach must have worked, because Cwmcarn Youth never took a backward step. On at least three occasions, two of them I admit may have had something to do with me, the entire team got sent off for fighting. Please take this the right way, but in my humble opinion that's what youth rugby was all about. We were a bunch of mates, who had grown up together, fighting through thick and thin together. Like young men going away to war together. The only difference being, our weapons were fists and boots.

I don't think we lost a game for about three years.

Yet youth rugby wasn't just about fighting on the field. It was all about the camaraderie off it as well. Drinking together, being top of that list.

Maybe it wasn't the best time to be courting. Many a Saturday night I promised to meet Steph at 7'o'clock. A few ciders and a sing-song later, 7pm turned into 8, 8pm to 9 and so on. If I had ten pounds for every time I said, 'Oh bugger it, I may as well be hung for a sheep as hung for a lamb' I would be a very rich man by now.

Instead, me and the boys would go to town on the pull. One night I got lucky with a girl two years older than me. An experienced piece of skirt! Outside the club we started necking. With her tongue exploring the inside of my mouth, I began feeling sick and my head started spinning. She certainly got more than than she'd bargained for when I spewed all over her. Warm cider and black all down the front of her dress. Not the most romantic thing I've ever done.

At 17 we got through to the Monmouthshire Youth Cup Final to face Newport Youth at Bedwas. Newport, being the bigger and more established club, regarded us as a bit of a joke, a bunch of rebels without a clue. They were probably right to think that. We didn't have club badges and ties. We were more like the evil twin of youth rugby. The dirty fifteen, in jeans, smoking Woodbines and necking cans of Strongbow.

On the Wednesday before the Friday night final, I again found myself up to no good. I told my girlfriend I was off to do some extra training and then we had an important team meeting. In truth, my mate, Pipper Watkins and I arranged to meet two girls from another village. I picked them up in my pride and joy, an old, beaten-up, Ford Anglia.

While driving on the M4, Pipper, sitting in the back seat behind me, decided to play night flying. A stupid game where he put his hands over my eyes until one of us chickened out. Me being me, and especially with two girls in the car, wasn't going to be the one to back down first. I could be a terrible show-off at times.

Both girls yelled at me to slow down. The girl in the front seat tried to pull Pipper's hands from my eyes. Laughing like a fool, Pipper didn't budge. Blindly, I kept going, faster and faster. Suddenly, he screamed and moved his hands away. The car headed straight towards a lorry. I panicked. I pulled the steering wheel sharply but lost control. The car shot up the bank. There weren't any crash barriers in those days. I pulled it back the other way. The car turned over and over. It ended the right way up, smashed to bits up against the central reservation. Other cars whizzed past. I thought we were all dead. Then the girls started crying.

The next thing to pop into my thick skull was, 'Shit! I'm going to miss the cup final.'

Thankfully, we all clambered up the bank to safety.

I couldn't believe that I had nearly killed everyone just for a dare, but that was how I was in those days. The car ended up a write-off, while I ended up in hospital with bruised ribs. The incident, and my name, made its way into the local newspaper, the South Wales Argus but I still managed to play in the final on the Friday. To be honest I would have tried to play even if I had broken my leg! We won it quite convincingly.

On the downside, my girlfriend wouldn't talk to me - not because of the accident, but because she had read in the newspaper about the other girls in the car.

Winning the cup final put our club in the shop window and lots of the boys went on to gain international youth caps while playing for Cwmcarn, which considering we were a small and unfashionable outfit, showed just how good we must have been. Unfortunately I wasn't one of those boys but looking back, that could have been of my own making. I did go for a Welsh Youth trial for East Wales, but as usual I messed up big style and got sent off, either for fighting or stamping or both, I don't remember. I just recall receiving an early bath and a message from the selectors, the first of many, to tell me not to darken their door again.

My free-and-easy life took an unexpected turn when Stephanie fell pregnant. I was 19 and she was a year younger. Not an ideal start to our lives, but we weren't the first and definitely wouldn't be the last to find ourselves in that situation.

Without a second thought, I fronted up and went to see her father. Fair play, he said I didn't have to marry her. Maybe he said it to get rid of me, but I decided that I wanted to do the right thing and put a ring on her finger.

Then came the more difficult part of going home to face my parents and telling them the interesting news.

I recall my father sitting in his chair, watching the TV.

'Can I have a word with you Dad?' I didn't want to beat about the bush. Beating the bush had got me into trouble in the first place! 'I've got Stephanie pregnant,' I blurted straight out.

He looked me up and down before muttering, 'I always knew your brains were in your bollocks.' That was it. His only words on the matter. He turned away from me and continued watching the box.

I then went into the kitchen to tell my mother I was getting married.

'When?' she asked.

'Probably very soon,' I replied.

'Oh dear,' she muttered, and then cracked a joke about buying a new dress and wondering what the nosey neighbours would say, and that was that.

We got married on a Thursday afternoon in a small chapel between Cwmcarn and Abercarn. A full Welsh wedding, with a room full of bad hairdos, terrible speeches, warm beer and dried-up sausage rolls. For our honeymoon we ventured all the way to the High Cliffs Hotel in sunny Bournemouth in my clapped-out Ford Escort van. It rained all week, so we mainly stayed in bed. Well that was our excuse!

For a short while we lived with Steph's grandmother in Cwmcarn. The house smelt of swede and dust but at least we had a roof over our heads. With another mouth to feed on the way, I needed to earn more money, so I resigned as the entertainment secretary for the Tin Works and went to work in Whitehead Bar Mill.

When Cathryn was born, it was the best thing that had ever happened in my life. A feeling only equalled by the birth of my second daughter, Nicola, a few years later.

Becoming a responsible parent proved such hard work, but was a great experience at the same time. It made me, well it made the both of us, grow up pretty quickly. I spent long hours in work to earn whatever money I could to ensure my family had everything they needed.

When Cathryn was a few weeks old, we moved in with Steph's parents. It proved to be a nightmare, well for me anyway. My father-in-law had always been pretty dominant in our lives, but at this point he just took over. He became much too influential for my liking. He seemed to be forever organising things for my wife and our daughter. At times I didn't feel in control of my own family. Maybe because I was still so young, he felt he was just helping out. Or perhaps he could see the writing on the wall between my wife and I from way back in those early days.

I couldn't wait for the day to come when we got our own place in Cwmcarn. When it finally came, the house was tiny but I didn't care, it was ours and I would love to think both my daughters would say they'd had very happy childhoods. I tried my best to be there for them. We had holidays abroad and did all the normal family stuff. I wanted to give them more love than my father had shown me at their age. I bought them whatever they wanted, but my wife Stephanie was the boss as far as my daughters were concerned. She was the one who laid down the law in our house. I don't ever remember giving them a row or telling them off.

When they had days off school I wanted to spend as much time as I could with them but with me working long hours, as well as the rugby training, it was difficult to fit it all in. Sometimes they would come with me in the truck, as long as it wasn't a long trip. It wasn't ideal, but at least I never made them fight other little girls in back lanes, and we did have some fun and quality time together on the odd trip now and again. We would stop on the way back for hot dogs or burgers. By the time we got back home they would normally be fast asleep in the cab cwtching up to their dolls. Really happy days for me.

Because my old man hadn't shown any interest in my education, I was adamant I would give my own children a better start in life so when they were old enough I sent them to private school. It cost an arm and a leg but it was well worth it. I wanted them to have a better education than I'd had.

One day I remember going to surprise Cathryn and Nicola by picking them up from school. Nicola came running excitedly towards me with a bottle of pop in her hand.

'Don't run,' I shouted.

But she fell over. The bottle smashed into her hand, cutting it to bits. There was blood everywhere. With my heart pounding, I rushed her to hospital where she had fifteen stitches. It broke my heart as it would with any father. I sat in A&E, tears running down my face, blaming myself for going to pick them up in the first place.

I may have been pretty tough when it came to smashing up other hookers and I have seen lots of blood, both on and off the field, including mine, but when it came to my own kids it was a different thing altogether. I felt dizzy and sick, angry and so sad. Lucky she got over it without any physical scars.

Another time, Cathryn came home from school really upset. She was about 12 or 13 years old at the time. I kept asking her what was wrong but she insisted that everything was okay. She locked herself in her bedroom, which was not like Cathryn at all. As a parent you just know when there is something upsetting your children. We finally got it out of her that she had been bullied in school. At the time, bullying was something people didn't really talk about.

To say I was mad would have been an understatement. Cathryn wouldn't tell us the bully's name. Like a lunatic, I drove straight to the school in my truck and demanded answers. After talking to the teachers I found out the girl's name.

As it happened, I knew the bully's father so I went straight to their house, steam coming out of my ears. No one touches my daughter! When I got there, the girl's mother wouldn't listen. She didn't accept it and started calling me a liar and saying it was probably my daughter's fault.

I don't know how I managed to keep control but I had a card up my sleeve. I grabbed the father's arm and took him to the bottom of the garden. 'I'm telling you now mate,' I stared at him. I didn't continue talking until he looked away. 'If my daughter gets bullied by your daughter ever again. If she even looks at her the wrong way, I will come looking for you...understand.' He nodded.

'Understand!' I poked him hard in the chest.

'Yes,' he murmured.

The bullying stopped.

Later in life, both my daughters became very close to my parents and visited them almost every Sunday for afternoon tea. Perhaps by then my father thought he would give them the time he hadn't given me or my sisters when we were growing up. To be fair, he was great with them.

One story we still talk about now was when my Mam and Dad were older and my father couldn't drive anymore, Nicola would take my mother shopping to Leo's supermarket in Pontllanffraith near Blackwood. My mother had false teeth that didn't fit too well and at the checkout her teeth fell out onto the conveyor belt. They slowly inched their way along the belt with a box of corn flakes, three pears and a bottle of toilet duck.

Nicola couldn't stop laughing. Fair play to my mother, she didn't panic and she didn't pick them up straight away. No, she waited until the dentures went to the end of the conveyor belt. Then she pulled out a wet wipe, cleaned them, put them back in her mouth and said to the cashier, 'Sorry about that love.'

I am so very proud of Cathryn and Nicola and their own families. Cathryn is now a sports teacher in Cardiff, while Nicola is a manager for Scottish and Southern Energy

Going back to just after Cathryn was born. Although married with a young child I was still looking forward to another year of youth rugby. But then a throwaway comment by my Dad changed all that. 'If you're doing things like a man,' he said, referring to me getting my girlfriend pregnant, 'you should act more like a man. Stop playing with kids and go and play with real men.'

Not wanting to show him any weakness. I looked him in the eye and replied. 'Ok....I will.'

My local village side, Abercarn, told me I could play for them but it would probably be for the Seconds. I'd watched the first team play a few times and, no disrespect, I knew I could hold my own in their company. They clearly weren't ready for a young upstart, straight out of the youth team, gate crashing their party.

'You've got to earn your stripes here, boy,' some old guy said to me.

The very next day I went three miles up the road to sign-up for a rival club, Crumlin. A crime paramount to treason in the Welsh Valleys. I'd heard tales of past players getting tarred and feathered just for watching rival clubs, never mind going to play for them. I half expected an angry mob to turn up at my house, holding torches, ready to burn me at the stake.

My mind had been made up and I didn't really care. Some of Crumlin's players said to me, 'Come up and we'll look after you', and that's just what they did! Some of the old heads took me under their wing. They had a lot to put up with mind. I was young and a little crazy and would strip naked at every opportunity. Unlike now, where I'm...well....older and a little wiser, but I still like to strip off.

Crumlin were a typical Valleys unit. A good robust side, full of characters that played hard and partied harder. In those days, we played lots of local derbies against the likes of Blaina, Pontypool United, and of course, Abercarn. Each game was like a cup final and we played for local bragging rights.

In a way it proved a good way to serve my front row apprenticeship, as there was always some old timer, who had just stepped down a level from Ebbw Vale or Tredegar or Pontypool or prison, a right tough old nut, hooking against me, or propping against us.

At times the games were brutal. Tough-as-teak miners or insane steel workers looking for a Saturday afternoon rumble and now and again, during a match, a spot of rugby would break out amongst all the fighting. I would be lying if I told you I didn't enjoy it. Eighty minutes of out and out violence. Blood, sweat and stud marks. Yet on the final whistle, every punch, boot and bite mark was forgotten. In the bar after I would always be with my opposite number sinking a few beers and having a *craic*.

Another big part of playing rugby for me was the opportunity to go away on tour. Over the years, the sport I love has given me the chance to travel the world several times over. Each one an opportunity to let my hair down and get myself into a whole load of mischief.

My first senior tour brings back great memories. We travelled all the way from rainy Crumlin to the glamorous destination of rainy Bradford. On the tour bus, on the way up, some of the established players warned me of the things they were going to do to me because it was my first trip away with them.

I'd been tipped-off by a mate that one of the things they always did to 'first timers' was to strip them naked, but I didn't mind that; in fact I was already naked and running around the bus when he was telling me. I would then be bundled into the back of a taxi, which didn't sound good, and taken somewhere miles away from the hotel before being kicked-out. Normally, in rugby circles, this was regarded as quite a funny thing to do to someone, unless of course that someone just happened to be you.

During the first few days of the tour my mind kept thinking of how I could get out of my initiation. I needed a plan. After discarding some stupid ideas, I decided the best option would be to roll a ten bob note up as tight as I could and carefully position it up the cheeks of my arse. The logic was at least I'd have some money to get a taxi back to the hotel. I did contemplate sticking a pair of underpants up there as well, but dismissed the idea for obvious reasons. One afternoon in my room I even practiced with the rolled up money, making sure it wouldn't fall out or that anyone could see it. Come the afternoon of the Kangaroo court, they did indeed strip me off, without much resistance I must add. They then bungled me into a waiting cab and with great delight, dumped me in the middle of a massive housing estate.

I ran around, by some shops, like a frightened rabbit, hands covering my crown jewels. People stopped and stared, more in shock than amusement, at the sight of a naked boy, running from doorway to doorway, frantically trying to flag down a taxi. Luckily an Asian driver stopped for me. He smiled at me as I sat there in the back of his cab and kept smiling at me throughout the journey. The grin soon disappeared from his face when I reached between my legs and handed him the rolled up ten bob note.

'Keep the change mate,' I said as I dashed out into the safety of my hotel.

All the players cheered when I strolled back into the room not that long after my kidnappers had got back. My first victory of the tour!

Just after my 21$^{st}$ birthday I passed my HGV class one license so I left the works at Whitehead and went to work for my father on the trucks.

I continued playing for Crumlin for around four years and played over two hundred games for the club. Although I'd won Player of the Year and felt I was doing well, no one from the next level of clubs came knocking my door. Maybe, getting sent off once or twice, or swinging from the light shades with my dick out every Saturday night, had tarnished my reputation, just a little. A few players in the club progressed up the ladder and went on to play for some of the local, first-class teams.

Disappointed, I kept plugging away. All my life I had been told by various individuals I wouldn't amount to anything in life. The more people told me this, the more I set out to prove them wrong. In a bizarre sort of way, I took inspiration in their negativity. So not getting selected to go and play for a bigger club, only made me even more determined to go and play for a bigger club.

Instead of feeling sorry for myself, I trained harder, and longer. I have always been a good trainer; even today I still train everyday. At Crumlin, after doing a real hard session, I always felt it was never enough. I would do double or triple what everyone else did. I'd go running, for miles, over mountains after work. I practiced throwing the ball in, hour upon hour. I wanted to prove to the doubters that they were wrong.

I wasn't a naturally gifted sportsman like a George Best or a Phil Bennett. So I worked at it. Numerous times throughout my career, I have been told I wasn't big enough to play for this club or that club, or that I was too much trouble, but I was never told I wasn't good enough. That spurred me on. I could make myself bigger and stronger. I could even bite my tongue on occasions and stay out of trouble. But I knew and so did others, that I was good enough if given the chance.

Then out of the blue, my chance came calling.

One cold, foggy, Wednesday night, the Crumlin team headed off to play Treherbert at the top end of the Rhondda. Our rickety old bus coughed and spluttered its way over the craggy, intimidating, Rhigos Mountain. Looking out of the window, I thought, 'One wrong move here and its curtains for all of us.' It made me think of that film, where an Argentinean rugby side crashed in a plane and ended up eating each other to survive. I looked around the bus wondering who I would eat first, the props or the committee men.

Anyway, Bob Bishop, one of the committee got up and called for order, 'Quiet down boys, I have an important thing to tell you.'

'You're gay?' I shouted.

'No, I'm not gay, Spikey, now shut up a minute,' he bellowed at me. 'One of our players has been asked to go train with,' he left a pause, 'Cardiff.'

There was a sharp intake of breath on the bus. Cardiff was the Manchester United of rugby at that time. Probably the biggest club side in the world, packed full of internationals and the odd British Lion or five.

'Jammy twat,' I thought, and looked about to see who it would be.

It took me, as much as everyone else, by surprise when Bob looked at me and said, 'It's you, Spikey.'

I honestly didn't have a clue.

Everyone cheered. Some patted me on the head. Others called me a Big City Ponce. That's Valley humour for you in a nutshell!

I didn't know what to think. The opportunity I wanted had unexpectedly been laid out in front of me but second thoughts and doubts quickly crept in. Don't ask me why but my first reaction was not to go. Maybe, I felt scared, but deep down I wanted it. I knew I was good enough; but what if it didn't work out? I knew of many a good player who had gone to the so-called big four clubs only to return, weeks later, with their tail firmly between their legs. I didn't want that! I couldn't cope with the rejection.

I sat there quietly, questions popping into my head. Did I really want to go? How was I going to get to Cardiff? What would I wear? At Crumlin, I was in my comfort zone with my mates. A big fish in a small pond. In Cardiff I would be more like a tiddler in the Atlantic Ocean in the middle of a raging storm, surrounded by tiddler-eating sharks.

'Don't be so stupid Spike,' my mates, Lawson Jones and Jeff Thomas said when I told them how I felt, 'you'll walk it.'

# 4

# Come in Cardiff - We Have Parity

## (whatever that means!)

*"No one trained harder and no one played harder. He had the heart of a lion. Small in stature but with a giant's presence."*

**Terry Holmes**
**Cardiff - Wales - British Lions**

That night, my head spun like a top. I hardly slept. The next day, Chris Padfield, a forwards coach at Cardiff, and schoolmaster at Newbridge Grammar School, phoned my house. He surprised me even more when he told me Cardiff had been to see me play a few times. They thought I was a very good player and wanted me to come down and start off by playing for their second side.

Although it was only the second team, this wasn't like playing for Abercarn Seconds. Cardiff Rags were probably the most famous second side in the country. A team that on their day could beat the first teams of many other top sides.

'We have three or four hookers, Michael,' Chris continued, 'some very good ones, so it's not going to be easy. We have one young lad who has just joined called Alan Phillips who already looks like he will definitely play for Wales one day.'

Dogs started barking. Birds flew out of the trees. The clock in my front room stopped. Even though I didn't know Alan from Adam, just the mention of his name sent a shiver down my spine. 'Is he now?' I thought to myself, 'I'll see about that. Unknowingly to Chris, or Alan, or even Adam, a challenge had been thrown down.

'Ok,' I said, 'when is training?' And the adventure began.

My wife and most of her family were rugby fanatics. Her uncle, a hard-as-nails collier, Steve Morris, won 19 caps for Wales from 1920 to 1925. Her father, also a Steve, went up to St Helens to play Rugby League in his twenties. Therefore, with rugby in her blood, Stephanie was made up when I told her about being asked to go training with Cardiff.

She wanted me to make such a good impression that she rushed out and bought me a new string vest and white underpants just for my first training session. It still makes me laugh thinking of it now.

I can imagine the Cardiff selectors talking about me after the training session had finished. 'What do you think of that Spikey character?'

'Well he didn't do much....but fair play, his string vest and pants looked fantastic. 100% pure cotton...and so...so white.'

My two daughters were old enough to understand what was going on. That night, they prayed that their Daddy would do well.

The following Monday, I travelled with Chris down to Cardiff. Later on in my career, even when I played at the highest level, I rarely got nervous about any game. However, I felt as scared as hell as we drove through the heavy city traffic. It's quite intimidating to go to any new rugby club, let alone one whose players I had watched on TV playing for their club, country, and the Lions.

As we pulled into the impressive Sophia Gardens complex

where they trained, I knew I was entering a whole different world. Even the changing rooms looked massive. I could actually walk about in them. If I had tied three cats together by their tails and swung them about, I still wouldn't have hit the player changing next to me. They were the complete opposite to changing in the shoe box-sized facilities at Crumlin where, on match days, some unlucky player (normally a back) would have to strip off in the showers.

At Cardiff, they even had different coloured training kits laid out, and bottles of water. They appeared so professional. However, what I recall most from my first session there, and probably the most disappointing thing about it, was that no one came up to talk to me. A room full of players, superstars and coaches but I may as well have been in a cell in Calcutta for murder. I sat alone in the corner getting changed. It seemed so strange, because they had asked me to go there and no one seemed to be bothered.

I did the session but my head was completely in the wrong place. I was outside my comfort zone and I didn't like it. I simply didn't make an impression. For the first time in my life I felt more than happy to just blend into the background like the trees surrounding the pitch. That wasn't me at all. When training in my home club, I was normally the star of the show. Cracking heads while cracking jokes.

In the car on the way home, I didn't say a lot. Chris didn't say much either. At home, my kids and wife waited for my return with smiling faces. The smiles fell to the floor when I threw my kit bag in the corner and announced, 'I'm never going back there again.'

I'm not blaming the fact I had under performed on nobody talking to me but it did have an effect. It was hard to take but I learnt a valuable lesson which stood me in good stead for the rest of my life, not just in rugby. Many years later, when I became the 'boss' at Cardiff and then at Newport, I wouldn't let anyone enter a changing room, or the club house, without going out of my way to talk to them. I would do anything to make whoever it was feel at home, I always made a fuss whether it was a big star or someone just stepping in to have the odd game. It didn't matter to me. Just asking them, "who they were? Where they came from"? I hoped it gave them the confidence to relax and enjoy it.

Chris called me the next night to ask how I felt. I thanked him for taking me there but told him it wasn't for me. My mind was made up, I was staying at Crumlin. The life of a rugby playing city slicker wasn't the life for me. I didn't want to talk about it anymore, I told him. My dream had faded away.

Like a true gentleman, Chris said he was shocked but understood. 'Look, its not easy,' he added, 'especially in a changing room with the likes of Gareth Edwards, Gerald Davies and Roger Lane. But please, please come to one more session. Just one more and if it doesn't work out, okay, we'll leave it be.'

I wouldn't budge. I was adamant I wasn't going again and that night I went to our usual training session with Crumlin. All the boys asked me how it went.

'Not my cup of tea.' I told them.

'Too hard for you Spikey?' someone asked.

The thing was, it hadn't been hard. I didn't find it physically hard at all. In fact, it was quite relaxed. While running in a group around the pitch, I started to go for it, and was more or less told to 'slow down son, and stay with the pack,' by some of the older heads. Physically I felt on the same level or even better than most of them, but mentality may have been the bigger problem.

One old guy sat in the corner of the Crumlin club with me after training. I'm still not sure if he was using some kind of reverse psychology, or if he genuinely meant what he said, as he bluntly stated, 'I didn't think you'd make it at Cardiff anyway, Spikey...It's too big a club for you!'

This was 'red rag to a bull' time again. If I didn't want to go, that was my choice, but no one was going to tell me they knew it wasn't for me. So, true to form, I ended up going. This time, however, it was shit or bust. If I failed it was going to be on my terms, no one else's. I wasn't going to roll over and blend into the background like before....Oh no!!

I glared around the Cardiff changing room. I thought, 'Superstars or not, I'm giving this my best shot. If it doesn't work out, so be it.'

With my proper head on, they didn't know what hit them. On the sprints, I took off like the Road Runner and finished about 20 metres in front of everyone else. The other players rolled their eyes and shrugged their shoulders. 'Slow down you nutter,' one of them yelled at me.

'Up yours,' I thought, 'I'm on a mission.'

At the end of the training session, we spilt into two teams to play a full contact game with the first fifteen (i.e. the Superstars) against the rest.

Showtime! I eyed them all up. This was my turn to shine. From the kick-off I smashed into every ruck and maul as if my life depended on it.

At their lineout on the halfway line I tensed like a greyhound in a cage waiting for the rabbit to be released. Their second row palmed it down to the great Gareth Edwards. In one movement he caught it and sent the ball away with a bullet pass, pure poetry in motion. The only problem for Gareth was that I'd never liked poetry. I sprinted around the line out and clothes-lined him. I nearly took his head off. We both clattered to the floor.

Everyone took a sharp intake of breath. I looked down, the

veins in my arms bulging. There I was, lying like a deranged banshee on top of the greatest rugby player the world had ever seen.

All I could hear was Gareth yelling 'Get this crazy fucker off me.'

I grinned at him, before someone pulled me up by the collar and tossed me away like a discarded chip paper.

'Well,' I thought, 'if I'm going to do it, I may as well put a top hat on the bloody thing.' I gave it my best shot.

After training, I sat alone in the cafe in Sophia Gardens eating some grub. Out of the blue, a big, black hand appeared in my face. The owner of which said, 'Hey do you mind if I sit by you?' It belonged to the impressive frame of Carl Smith, the first black guy to ever play for the Welsh Youth. At first I thought he was going to tell me off for what I did, or even beat me up. He looked around and whispered, 'Hey! That was great what you did to Gareth. I've been waiting for someone to do that for ages!' The smile on his face was as wide as the River Taff.

'Thanks, but I think I might have messed my chances up.'

'No way. You wait and see. You done good.'

Next, Ian 'Robbo' Robertson, who later became a lifelong friend, came over and joined us. Soon other players flocked around me. The new kid had impressed them. In hindsight, maybe I should have pulled Gareth's head off and kicked it over the goalposts at my first training session. Then they may have accepted me from the start.

The great Gareth stayed well away mind you. On saying that, I soon got on really well with the genius Welsh scrum-half, and still do. I often see him at functions all over the world and with a wry grin he always recalls the first time we 'bumped' into each other.

I felt much better about Cardiff after that and decided to

give it a go. Overnight, I went from the crazy hooker playing for Crumlin, to the crazy hooker running out for the biggest team in Wales. Quite a big achievement back in my village.

Within a fortnight I found myself firmly in the Cardiff set up and on my way to London to play against another massively famous club. Both the first and second teams, went up to play London Welsh before the England v Wales, Five Nations International. Like all rugby clubs, the more established players sat at the back of the coach, or on the seats with tables, playing cards. I sat down the front on my tod, excited but still wondering what the hell I was doing there. I'd come from Crumlin where I had been more or less the 'cock of the walk'. Now, I felt more like a feather duster for sure, but I knew it wouldn't take me long.

The first team played on the one pitch, and we played simultaneously on the other but there were more people watching our game than had ever watched me before. With all the added pressure I couldn't remember the line-out signals. My mind went completely blank. The more I concentrated the worse it got. Robbo stormed over. 'What's wrong, Spikey?'

'The planes, the planes are putting me off.' I sounded like the small guy from Fantasy Island.

We both looked up at the sky. 'Are you bloody serious?' Shaking his head he walked away.

The nerves had got to me so much, I blamed the aeroplanes flying above my head for the confusion. Other than that little mishap, I didn't have a bad game.

Once my confidence was up it didn't take long to establish myself, both on and off the field. I hadn't even stripped naked yet, but that wouldn't take me long. After a few games for Cardiff Rags I forced myself into the senior squad. My first game happened to be in Italy. I couldn't believe it. One minute I was playing against Treherbert on a wet Wednesday night and then, less than a month later, I was sat on a plane going to Rome to meet the Pope. Ok, not the Pope. The Roman Catholic Church warned me not to go within five hundred yards of his Holiness! But I was off to Italy all the same.

On a serious note, Alan Philips and I had leap-frogged the other hookers in the club to go on the trip. We played two games. I played against a select Italian side, up in the mountains of L'Aquila. The other game, which Alan got picked for, was against the full Italian side at the Olympic Stadium in Rome. It wasn't like the Italian team of today, but they were still a tough old unit.

In my game I scored my first try for Cardiff. I ran about 20 yards from the front of the line-out to touch down. Of course as the night progressed, and the wine flowed, my try got further and longer with every glass. By the time I got back to my village, it had been a length of the field wonder try, side-stepping 40 players while blowing kisses to a beautiful Italian princess in the crowd.

My performance on the field, and my comic routines off it, definitely got me a firm foothold on the ladder with the senior squad. Even though I didn't play in the game in Rome, I was on the bench as a replacement, the trip opened my eyes to a brand new world, and the squad's eyes to the wonder of Spikey.

Then, like everything in life, it came crashing down to earth with a bump. From the warmth of Italy, it was back to the cold and unfriendly atmosphere of South Wales club rugby. With Cardiff being the team to beat and me being new to the team, I found myself being targeted by our opponents. During one game against Aberavon, as I packed down for the first scrum and just before our scrum-half put the ball in, their prop, John Richardson, moved his head slightly and spat straight in my face. I could feel his phlegm on my cheek.

'You dirty bastard,' I yelled. I turned to butt him and lost the ball against the head, which was sacrilege for a hooker at any level, never mind one playing first-class rugby. Only when he grinned at me did I realise he knew exactly what he was doing. At the next scrum, the same thing happened. I had to make a choice and quickly. Either get covered in gob at each scrum, or whack him.

It wasn't a hard decision. I threw a punch but missed him by a whisker. It had the desired effect though, because he stopped gobbing at me. Funny enough, John played for Wales a few years later and we became great friends.

Then again, I didn't have it all my own way. I learnt a real hard lesson three games later. I had come back from a slight injury and played for Cardiff Athletic against Gloucester's second team on the Arms Park. I was most probably being a pain and throwing my weight about. Before long, both packs broke-up and squared-up to each other. When the ref turned his back on us, the Gloucester prop Phil Blakeway, punched me square on the nose. He caught me a good one. Tears filled my eyes. I saw stars, the lot. The crowd cheered.

'Ref,' I grunted, 'did you see that.'

He shrugged his shoulders.

My worst nightmare; I even had to go off for treatment. The bastard had broken my nose. Patched up, I raced back on. Full of bravado, I said to Phil, 'Oh mate, is that the best you can do?' With that he gave me another one on exactly the same spot.

The crowd cheered louder. I rocked back but didn't go down. I snarled at him. He winked at me. Even my own players had a wry smile. It taught me a lesson, When you have taken a good punch on the nose or anywhere, just keep your mouth shut, and bide your time.

I refused to go off. I stayed on the field with cotton wool rammed up my broken nose. After the game, Phil and I had a few beers and a laugh about it. I played against him many times after, but never did get my own back. No wonder he went on to play for England.

In my early years at Cardiff, Gerald Davies, a Welsh hero and a true gentleman, was captain of the club. When he gave his team talk before each game he never swore, and never lost his temper. His favourite word was 'parity'. He would always say to us forwards, 'Look guys, as long as we get parity everything will be good.'

Everyone in the changing room sat there nodding their heads in agreement. Like the rest, I nodded along like those toy dogs you see in the back of cars. But to be honest, I really didn't know what he was going on about. I didn't know what 'parity' meant. This went on game after game. I didn't like to ask anyone else what it meant, just in case they thought I was duller than I looked.

It bugged me so much, I had to find out, so I plucked-up the courage to ask some of the other boys.

'God knows Spike,' replied David Barry.

'I haven't got a clue, but it sounds good,' said Terry Holmes.

I asked two others. They didn't know either. One of them actually thought it was to do with having a party. Then some clever clogs chipped in, 'Don't you know what it means?'

'I wouldn't be asking you if I did. So what does it mean.' I grunted back.

In the end, it panned out that he didn't know either. I guess it showed that either we were all as thick as two short planks or Gerald Davies was super intelligent, or a bit of both.

But we all agreed it must have meant something important, because Gerald used the phrase every bloody game.

David volunteered to find out by the next training session. 'Parity', he enlightened me, 'is the state or condition of being equal, esp. regarding status or pay.' He read it parrot-fashion from a piece of paper he'd copied out of the dictionary.

David could have said anything, and I wouldn't have known any different.

Information was power. So the next game, when Gerald set off on his "parity march", we all smiled to each other. Now I knew what he was harping on about, I listened with intent to his team talk. When we ran out of the tunnel for the game I made sure I ran out behind Gerald. In the tunnel, I tapped our captain on the shoulder. He turned around. Brimming with confidence, I proudly said, 'We'll get more than parity today Gerald, that's for sure!'

He looked at me and smiled. 'Well done, Spikey,' he said, as if I was a little kid in nursery who had used the potty for the first time without making a mess on the floor.

I ran out on that field feeling ten feet tall. 'Parity' was now my middle name. I got sent off in the first three minutes. No, I didn't, but that would have been a great ending to that story.

The more matches I played for the star-studded Cardiff team, the more my game improved. At 23 years of age, I felt a completely different player to the one who had run out every Saturday for Crumlin. Some of my team mates called me The Mole, for my ability to burrow into mauls and come out with the ball.

Then something unbelievable happened. From out of nowhere, I got selected to play for Wales B team against the French at Pontypool Park in 1976. After only about a half dozen games for Cardiff's first team I was now in the Welsh set up. I couldn't believe it. Like I said, I'd never won any youth caps and hadn't been in the system before. It probably wouldn't happen today. Nowadays, players go from a small club to a bigger club and progress to play for one of the regional sides before they get anywhere near the Welsh squad. Most of today's players get groomed through the Rugby Academy system. I'm not sure if the system would allow it to happen these days. I felt like the Spikey 'Rocky' Balboa of Welsh rugby.

When I first heard, I thought they had mixed me up with someone else. Or someone was playing a practical joke on me. I double checked. It was true. My name printed there in black and white alongside nine other newcomers plus some old heads like Clive Burgess, Jeff Squire and David Burcher, the Newport centre who was the captain.

The game itself was lost in a blur. It went so fast I can't recall much about it, except we beat them convincingly 24 points to 6. On saying that, I do recollect how big, nasty and ugly the French forwards were. It looked like their mothers had beaten them around the head with shovels when they were born. They didn't get any prettier over the following years. In fact, they only seemed to get bigger, nastier and a lot uglier. The senior French team looked like their mothers, fathers, and their grandparents, had beaten them with shovels when they were born. All at the same bloody time!

The day after the game, however, I felt disappointed, but not too dissatisfied. It had been an unexpected experience but I didn't think anything more would come of it. On my first game back for Cardiff after winning my first B cap, I played a low-key, nothing sort of game, in the reserves against Pontypool United and got sent off. Banned for four, long weeks after decking some fat prop who had been determined to nail me first. I felt gutted. Cardiff weren't happy. We'd had a spate of players sent off in a few weeks.

At least the ban enabled me to earn some well-needed money again with my proper job. Being self-employed and playing rugby at that level had its downside as well as its ups. Rugby was very much an amateur sport. We may have had a few free beers to celebrate a victory after a game, but try paying the rent or the electric bill or buying the kid's Christmas presents with a handful of beer tokens.

By then I was working for my old man's haulage business. I even had my own truck. The work took me all over the country to Leeds, Manchester and London. It was getting increasingly difficult because my rugby career was really starting to take off.

Asking some old docker to hurry up and unload the truck because I had training in a few hours, didn't cut much ice. It wasn't the ideal preparation to sit in the cab, driving for five or ten hours a day, then rush back for training. But I did that, day after day, for well over ten years. That's just the way it was back then. Rugby was my passion but it didn't put bread on the table. In fact, it often took it off because I couldn't work weekends or overtime in the week of an important match.

Most training nights, I wouldn't have time to go home after work to get changed. Instead, I took my kit bag with me in the truck. I'd rush back from wherever I had been delivering to or picking up from, straight to training. I used to back my truck up on the ramp in front of the Old Arms Park. I'd leap out and go training. Today it makes me smile to myself when I see famous footballers and rugby players in their top-of-the-range sports cars or Range Rovers driving into training with the TV cameras blanking out their registrations. There I was rolling up in a 36-ton Volvo 88 lorry with 'Arthur J Watkins' plastered over the side.

To be fair to Cardiff, they would have let me park on the field if I had wanted. They appreciated the effort I made to get there. Some of the other team members lived in Cardiff, didn't work, and still turned up late for training.

One Friday afternoon, Terry Holmes and myself drove to London to get a load of scrap. Due to one thing and another, I ended up sleeping in the cab for the night, while Terry slummed it in some terrible doss house near Swindon. The next day we were playing against the mighty Leicester at the Arms Park. So at first light, we bombed it back to Wales, unloaded, mainly by hand, 30 tons of scrap, then drove to the ground and played the game. And we bloody beat them!

On another occasion, I found myself working in the Swansea area. That Wednesday evening we were playing Llanelli down at Stradey Park so, with no chance of getting home in time or of meeting the coach in Cardiff, I drove straight to the ground. It made sense anyway since I was down that way. I got there really early, way before the team coach had turned up. It had been an early start for me so I parked up behind the stand and had a kip in the bed in the back for an hour. When the boys turned up, Terry woke me up and I went in to change. Playing Llanelli was always a big tense affair and, really focussed, I raced out on the field like a terrier. Suddenly, over the tannoy system the announcer said, 'Would the owner of vehicle number TR43 4QB please move your truck? You are parked in the Chairman, the Secretary, the Committee men, and the visitor's car park spaces.' We could all hear his voice cracking as he tried to hold back the laughter.

Everyone in the crowd burst out laughing. I must have 'accidentally' parked it across the front of the clubhouse, unknowingly, honest! But I couldn't move it then could I? They would have to wait. Walking into the clubhouse later, all the Llanelli committee glared at me as if I was Satan himself.

My truck and I became well known at rugby clubs up and down the land for many a year. Doing such an unpredictable job while playing rugby for a top class team was a struggle, but it became part and parcel of my life.

The daily toil proved to be well worth it when, again out of the blue, I got a call asking me to go and train with the main

Welsh squad. Some still say the greatest team Wales ever had. A team that had won the Grand Slam the year before, 1976, without breaking sweat. The golden generation of players I had watched on TV ripping sides apart with the likes of Gareth Edwards, Phil Bennett, JPR, and Mervyn Davies.

How did I feel? For the first time in my life I sat in my kitchen speechless. This was beyond my wildest dreams. Like I said, I'd never been close to playing for Wales at any level. Now, suddenly, I would be sitting in the same changing room with most of my heroes.

Many people in Wales were completely surprised by my inclusion. I was flabbergasted myself. I can only imagine what Alan Phillips thought. I bet he spat Sugar Puffs all over his Superman pyjamas when he read about it in the Western Mail. Like I said, in Cardiff's eyes, he was the next big thing, the high-class hooker on the street corner until I turned up in 6 inch, studded, Patrick Stilettos.

Whether I deserved it or not, I didn't care, I was going for it. From the very first minute of my very first training session, I felt at home in that company. We trained down at the Afan Lido in Aberavon. The sessions were very intense, with lots of contact. We used to scrummage on the beach. We didn't have fancy scrummaging machines like they have today. Three hours or more of pure, hard, physical graft, pack against pack. No holds barred. More than once it ended up in a full-on fist fight after someone had thrown the odd haymaker.

Violence wasn't actively encouraged, but the coaches didn't mind a bit of fisticuffs now and again. They would be standing on the sideline, rubbing their hands. Two packs of lions scrapping it out in the sand. I think they believed it was a way of team bonding.

The pack at that time was full of hard blokes. The Pontypool front row, Geoff Wheel, Allan Martin, Derek Quinnell and

Trevor Evans, to name a few. I had to quickly stand up for myself otherwise I would have been ground into the dirt.

Funny enough, that year when Wales won the Grand Slam, some newspaper reporter asked Charlie Faulkner, 'Who had been the hardest pack they had faced in the competition?' In good old Charlie style he drawled, 'The side we packed down against in training.'

Later in my life, when I went on to coach teams like Pontypridd, I tried to replicate the same intensity. I'd have two packs smashing into each other at each session. To me, nothing beats doing it for real, maybe with a bit of violence thrown in. As long as it was strictly controlled violence, and it stayed on the field.

Being in the Welsh set up was one thing but getting off the bench and winning an actual cap proved a lot tougher. The biggest hurdle I faced came in the shape of Bobby Windsor. He had been the Welsh hooker for ages, a British Lion and of course a member of the world famous Pontypool front row. Not only were they a formidable unit, they were also a global brand, like Coca Cola or Heinz Beans, especially after Max Boyce had penned a song about them.

*Up and Under here we go,*
*Are you ready, yes or no?*
*Up and Under here we go,*
*It's the song of the Pontypool Front Row*

What the hell would have happened if I had broken the trio up? What would poor Max had sung instead for the last line.

*It's a song about two Pontypool Front Rowers and the nutter from Abercarn.*

Somehow it didn't have the same ring to it.

I replaced Roy Thomas, the poor sod from Llanelli. He had kept the bench warm for 36 games and the only cap he got, was a Kiss-me-Quick hat in Blackpool. Bobby just refused to go off and I don't blame him for that at all.

It wasn't like it is today. Modern rugby teams use at least 108 subs in each game. In those old days, a player's head had to be hanging off before they even brought on a stretcher. And then the player had to get examined by a doctor to confirm they couldn't carry on before a sub would even think about getting stripped off.

What didn't help me at all was that there had never been any love lost between Bobby and myself. We didn't get on from our early days. It had nothing to do with him keeping me out of the team. I'd known Bobby for a long time. I played against him when he played for Cross Keys and me at Crumlin. I worked in Whiteheads steel works, the same works as him and Charlie. So I often saw him outside rugby circles as well.

In my opinion, Bobby was all talk with little action. On top of that, I wouldn't bow down to him. From that first training session, I looked him squarely in the eyes. I gave him as good, or even better, than he gave me. He knew I didn't respect him or his hard man reputation.

I would like to think he saw me as his biggest threat. Whenever someone asked him who the best hookers in Wales were, he would mention everyone except me. Knowing Bobby, I took that as a compliment. He would never have talked about anyone he knew was any good.

However, I still sat on the bench, game after game. It was tough. There I was, building myself up for possibly the biggest day of my life, only to find myself frustrated by not getting on the field. It felt so disappointing when the final whistle blew. After a while I knew exactly how poor Roy, and his wife, felt!!

I'm not ashamed to admit, it got to a point where I prayed for Bobby to get injured. Nothing serious mind, just two broken legs and his head left hanging on by his tongue, or maybe for him to get kidnapped and chained to a radiator for a couple of years by a group of fanatical, Rugby Fundamentalists. Where was that bloody Pontypool groundsman with his bucket of lime when I needed him?

I just had to grin and bear it. I was still young enough to wait in the wings and just to be there was a great experience. Playing a small part as the team won the third Grand Slam of the decade in 1978, and our third consecutive Triple Crown.

My club form went from strength to strength. One time I faced Bobby and the rest of the 'Pooler' pack in a cup game at Pontypool Park. Even though our pack got destroyed, I had one of my best games ever. I completely outshone Bobby. I never lost a single ball against the head and around the field I popped up everywhere. I even gave Gerald Davies, who scored four tries that day, the scoring pass for us to win the game in the dying minutes.

'How's that for fucking parity Gerald?' I asked knowingly, as we jogged back to the halfway line.

After the match, a selector told me I would definitely be on the plane for the up-coming Welsh summer tour in May and June to Australia . The great Phil Bennett, Gareth Edwards and a few others had retired. It was time to rebuild the team.

Putting aside the loss of wages to cover the two months trip I couldn't wait to fly to Oz. It would be my first big trip away with Wales. I felt so proud and honoured to be flying to the other end of the world to represent my country.

In my mind, I'd imagined all of us players slumming it in First-Class. I couldn't wait to tuck into all that champagne and caviar. We'd probably all have head massages from the air hostesses and perhapy a 'happy ending' thrown in for luck. Only joking!

Champagne and caviar be buggered. Definitely only in

my wildest dreams. Even though Wales were one of the most successful sporting teams around, full of world class superstars, they made us travel cattle class. On top of that, we flew more or less straight through. One quick stop to refuel in Bombay, and we were off again.

Of course, the bigwigs relaxed up the front, sampling the free champagne and ogling the air hostesses. But deep down I didn't care. I wouldn't have minded if they had given me a pair of welding goggles and strapped me to the wing. I was 'over the moon with a golden spoon' just to be on the trip of a lifetime, playing the game I loved.

During the flight I sat next to Terry Holmes and Stuart Lane. Squashed into two small seats opposite us like two, huge, grizzly bears, sat Geoff Wheel and Charlie Faulkner. Geoff suffered terribly from Saint Vitus Dance which caused him to shake, rattle and roll at the most awkward of times.

Every time the air stewardess walked past, Geoff's head shook violently and his entire body rocked back and forth. He looked like a patient from the movie, *One Flew over the Cuckoo's Nest*. Scared stiff, she would jump back. I'm not sure if she thought he was doing it on purpose. It looked so sad but bloody hilarious at the same time.

Half an hour into the flight, she asked the two old dinosaurs what they wanted to drink.

'A gin and tonic,' replied Charlie, 'A nice G&T would be lovely.'

Geoff nodded his head. I didn't know if he wanted the same as Charlie or his affliction had kicked in again. She quickly returned with two drinks for them and had only just turned her back when both the drinks had gone. Charlie sat there licking his lips. I'm not sure if Geoff drank his or accidentally threw it over the man behind him.

Me and Terry sat watching and giggling like two schoolboys

at the back of the class. Charlie sat there clicking his fingers at the poor woman every ten minutes or so. 'Two more love,' he yelled.

This went on several more times with Charlie beckoning for her attention by shouting or clicking his fingers. In the end the overworked hostess whispered to Charlie, 'Look sir, next time you want a drink just press the button above you head.'

Charlie looked up at the series of buttons above his head. 'Oh, ok, I didn't know that. That's a good idea.'

Minutes later, Charlie's voice boomed down the plane. 'Oh... Oh...Oh Love,'

'What's the problem?' she said.

'It's this love.' Holding his glass up against the overhead buttons, Charlie was pushing it as if it was an optic on the top shelf of a bar, 'It's not working, there's no drink coming out of it. It must be empty.' He thought the gin and tonic was going to come through the button. Not that she had meant for him to just push the button to call her.

I laughed so much I thought I was going to wet myself. 'Bloody hell Terry,' I said, 'what have we let ourselves in for?'

When we landed after the 30 hour flight, there was none of this chilling-out in the swimming pool for a day or two, no way! We were straight into hard training in Perth the next day. Pack against pack, fighting on the beach.

When we did get some time for ourselves, the reception we received from the people of Perth was second to none. They invited us to BBQs, yacht racing, partying at fancy clubs: with all the beer we could drink.

Nevertheless, my reputation for being a little bit of a loose cannon had preceded me. Clive Rowlands, the team manager, and John Dawes, the coach, who I always called Jack Dawes followed by a Whaa Whaa, kept warning me to behave and stay out of trouble.

One night before an official function, they summoned me into their room.

'Spikey, this is a big do tonight. We want you to behave.'

'Of course,' I said in my best 'butter wouldn't melt in my mouth' voice.

'To keep an eye on you,' Clive added, 'I want you to bring me drinks all night.'

I thought he was joking at first. He wasn't. 'Come on Clive, I want to enjoy myself as well.'

Even though I think he liked me deep down, he still didn't trust me. 'Spike, no buts, I want you to bring me a gin and tonic every quarter of an hour.'

'But!'

'Spikey!' He just gave me a look.

'OK!' I sloped out of the room, thoroughly pissed off. Then the little devil appeared on my shoulder. It whispered into my ear. 'Right then, if Mister Rowlands wants a gin and tonic every quarter of an hour tonight, a gin and tonic every quarter of an hour, he will have.'

Some of the boys agreed to help me.

When I gave him the first gin and tonic, he sat there in his blazer and dickie bow, grinning like a Cheshire cat. Fifteen minutes later, on the dot, another one appeared on the table in front of him. He laughed and made a joke to the people around him about his new manservant.

I carried out his command to the letter of the law. At one stage, he waddled off to the toilet, probably to throw up. I waited. Fifteen minutes later, I climbed up on the seat of the next cubicle and handed down to him his new gin and tonic.

'Stop it Spikey, wait till I come out.'

'I am only doing what you said Clive.' I was on a mission. Like a programmed robot. I wouldn't stop. The boys sat there pissing themselves.

And it didn't stop when the function ended. I waited until he went to bed, then I rapped on his door. 'Your gin and tonic, Clive?'

I could hear him moaning in the room. Even though I was knackered, I stayed awake all night, banging on his door every fifteen minutes. By the morning there was a line of full drinks outside his hotel room.

He never asked me to be his man servant again! On the other hand, I didn't get into any trouble that night. So maybe his plan had worked.

On the playing front, we knew it was going to be a tough trip. We had been shown videos of how they had beaten the English team up a year before. It had been real, premeditated, thuggery of the highest order. From the kick-off they had piled into 'The Poms' and the Aussie refs had turned a blind eye.

We agreed, man for man, they weren't going to roll us over so easily.

I played all the mid-week games, often packing down with two thirds of the infamous Pontypool front row. 'Get that song ready Max!' I thought.

One of the big mid-week games of the tour was against Queensland and my excitement was bubbling-up like a bottle of pop. Peter Horton, their hooker, and I, eyeballed each other from the off. It was simply a case of not if, but when, it was going to kick off. Adrenalin flowed through my veins at 100 miles per hour.

At the first lineout, down in the far corner in Ballymore, Horton screamed at the ball boy. He gave him some nasty abuse because he reckoned the boy hadn't given him the ball quick enough.

'You horrible bastard,' I thought, 'making the poor boy feel really small in front of everyone.' I bet his parents were in the crowd as well. It had probably been a really proud moment for them.

It shouldn't have mattered to me how he treated one of his own, but I was so hyped up this was the perfect excuse. As Horton went to throw the ball in, I walked-up and lumped him on the side of the head as hard as I could. He went down like a sack of spuds. Everything kicked off, big style. Players raced at me throwing punches. I stood my ground. The rest of our pack, plus Terry Holmes, stood toe-to-toe by my side. When it all cooled down, I don't think the ref could believe what he had seen. He gave me a quick telling off and let the game carry on, which was a real surprise, since the ref, Bob Burnett, from Queensland, did his best throughout the game to let them win.

Calling him a no-good, one-eyed, referee would have been an understatement. He even wore the same coloured maroon and white socks as the region.

At one lineout I asked, 'Who's ball is it, ref?'

He replied, 'Ours!'

But even playing against sixteen men, somehow we won, and took their three-year-old unbeaten ground record. It wasn't the last we saw of Mister Burnett. His appointment to take charge of the First Test had us packing our bags and nearly flying home. It would have been like letting Max Boyce referee a game between Wales and England in Glynneath!

A massive diplomatic row erupted. The players and Clive Rowlands, to be fair to him, decided to go home. We were about to leave for the airport when another emergency meeting was called. Two hours later an unhappy Clive informed us that the WRU had not only refused to back us, but were demanding that we play the match whatever happened, or else! That threat made a lot of us very angry.

The tests were tough enough, with or without their homemade, slightly-biased, referees and we ended-up losing both of them. In the Second Test, Steve Finnane, the Wallaby prop, punched Pricey from behind and broke his jaw. A real cheap shot. What made it worse was that from where I was sitting our so-called hard men like Bobby Windsor didn't want to know. The only one to have a real go back was Clive Davis from Newbridge.

Away from the rugby, I enjoyed the little time off we had to ourselves. Off the field, the more established players, who had been in the set-up through the glory years, hung-out together. This left us new recruits to make our own fun.

That's not saying it was all, us and them. I got on well with most of the squad. There were a couple of odd characters, but they didn't bother me, and I didn't bother them. I loved Ray Gravell. He was a great guy, and I know he liked me. We had the same passion for Wales even though he came from the West and me from the East.

He always used to shout out, 'Spikey bach, calon, calon!' A term of endearment about how big my (calon) heart was.

I also got on very well with the likes of the Panther, alias Allan Martin, Geoff Wheel, Derek Quinnell, John Richardson from Aberavon, Steve Fenwick and a few others.

Yet, of everyone I've met playing rugby; I got on like a house on fire with Charlie. A friendship was formed on that tour which survived the test of time and is still as strong today as ever. In many ways, he was my biggest inspiration. My biggest fan, my best mate and the man who has made me laugh out loud, without even trying, more than anyone else in the world. (You will find out more later....a lot more!)

So, us young guns, me, Terry Holmes, Stuart Lane, John Richardson, Barry Clegg and Clive Davis made our own entertainment. In Sydney, a friend of Clive's, a guy by the name of John Blackborrow, originally from Newport, invited us out on his boat.

We waited excitedly in the sunshine of Sydney Harbour. There was no sign of him. We were just about to leave when a fog horn sounded and the big, smiling face of John sailed towards us. We clambered aboard. It wasn't very big, but large enough for all of us to have a tour of Sydney harbour while sampling the mandatory bucket of ice-cold beers. Once we'd done the Opera House and Sydney Harbour Bridge we were looking for something else to keep us amused.

'I know where there is a great nudist beach, Lady Jane Beach' John piped up. 'It's not far around the coast. All in favour say "Aye."

As you can imagine, there were more 'Ayes' than you could shake a stick at.

So we set off. About an hour, and quite a few cans of beer later, John anchored the boat about 200 metres off-shore. Looking at the action on the beach, I thought I had died and gone to heaven. While growing up I was used to going to Barry Island, where even in the height of summer, women wore coats and head scarves. Now, everywhere I looked, I could see tits, arses and knobs bouncing about, but not on the same people I must add. Beautiful young people played volleyball or other beach games in the nude. One old fisherman sat on the rocks with his knob out. I'm not sure if he was trying to use it as bait.

All the boys decided I should be the one to go ashore to check things out. Ok, maybe I suggested that I should be the one to go ashore to check things out. Anyway, they didn't disagree, so I completely stripped off and swam ashore. Minutes later, I stood on the beach with my pride and joy swinging about in all its glory.

I wandered about for a while, trying to join in with their games, but they didn't want to know me. Suddenly I heard the sound of a boat engine starting up and laughing and waving as my mates sailed away. I thought they were messing and would soon turn around and come back. No chance. I went running down the beach after them as the boat disappeared out of sight.

They left me there, alone on the beach, naked, for hours. It turned out all was not lost because I managed to make some new friends before the end of the day. A few girls gave me their telephone numbers and said I should call them. Result!

As the sun dropped, most people left for the day. By that time, it was getting dark, and cold. Good job those girls who gave me their numbers had gone by then.

I didn't know what I was going to do. Maybe go up on the road and hitch a lift, but I didn't have any clothes. I sat on a rock calling my mates every name under the sun, which by then had more or less disappeared. Then our boat appeared in the distance. All the guys stood on the deck, laughing like hell and obviously very drunk. I had the last laugh however as I contacted my nudist friends for a few beers the next day, and enjoyed whatever else was on the menu.

In the true spirit of meanness, the scroungers at the WRU wouldn't let us phone home to our wives and families unless we paid for the calls ourselves. Calling someone in London from Abercarn was expensive enough. Phoning home from the other side of the world would cost an arm, a leg and a bloody kidney.

Faced with this some players resorted to dirty tricks. One unnamed player asked the owner of a restaurant, who had supplied us with free drinks most of the afternoon, if he could use the phone to call the hotel. Instead, he rang home and cost the restaurant owner at least a couple of kidneys.

Like I mentioned, Charlie and I became very close on that tour. Partners in Wine! Like an old fox, Charlie was always thinking of ways to get one over on the powers-that-be. After training one day, in Brisbane, we waited in the team meeting room for the usual debrief. There was only me and Charlie there at the time. Charlie looked about and said, 'Hey, I have an idea. We can ring home from here. Watch the door Spike. I'll book it on John Dawes' room.'

'Good idea,' I mocked, 'Jack Dawes' room...Whaa...Whaa.' I guarded the door

He picked up the house phone, got through to the hotel switchboard and barked out his home number in Newport.

'To whom do I charge the call?' asked the operator.

'Err...Mister Dawes. John Dawes,' mumbled Charlie.

'Whaa...Whaa,' I bellowed out in the background.

Charlie glared at me.

'Please remain by the phone for a moment, Mr. Dawes, and I'll call you back,' came the reply.

Charlie replaced the receiver. By the time the call came through a few minutes later, more players had come into the room.

'Ullo,' said Charlie.

'I have a call to Newport in South Wales for Mister John Dawes,' confirmed the operator.

Charlie took a quick look around. 'Sorry love, he's not here,' he barked, and hung up.

'Charl....that was your wife, you idiot.'

'Oh bloody hell.' He shrugged his broad shoulders.

The incident which still makes me laugh today involved the team and a Koala bear on the rampage. The Welsh centre, Steve Fenwick was a well established star. A bit of a loveable rogue, with a real wicked streak, he was always playing tricks on players, and especially on committee men.

One day we were having a photo shoot in some wildlife park. Due to his model good looks, the photographer picked Steve to be at the centre of the shot holding a Koala bear. The rest of us looked like extras from a bad Spaghetti Western movie, with our broken noses and cauliflower ears. And not even the good extras. We were the extras that get shot in the first scene.

The animal trainer then placed the Koala carefully in Steve's arms. I was surprised how big it was. The size of a medium sized dog. While Steve held it, the trainer stood just out of shot, trying to keep the creature quiet by feeding it eucalyptus leaves now and again. On the other side, our trainer stood with a can of Fosters and a long straw, to make sure Steve was quiet.

Once they got in position, the photographer asked some of us to come into the shot.

I ripped all my clothes off and rushed in. No, I didn't, I had learnt my lesson from the boat trip. Me, fully clothed, and Terry stood either side of Steve ready for the photo. Steve was a little apprehensive. The bear looked cuddly enough but I imagined that if someone upset it, it would go bonkers.

Unluckily for Steve, on that particular day I was in the 'upsetting a bear' kind of mood. I cautiously placed my hand around the bear's back. While I stood there smiling away, I felt something warm near my fingers. It was the bear's arsehole. Without a second thought, I stuck my finger right up the koala bear's hole. The bear went berserk. It leapt all over Steve, ripping his jacket and his shirt more or less off his back. Its claws tore straight through to his skin.

'Get him off me...get him off me.' In panic, Steve dropped it on the floor. It's a wonder he didn't drop-kick the thing over the trees.

The bear went for him again. I quickly got out of the way whilst the bear's handler struggled to get the irate animal under control. Steve stood there, his face white, his clothes ripped to shreds. Visibly shaken, the trainer turned to Steve and said, 'Sorry...Sorry but he's never done that before.'

I thought, 'He's probably never had a Welsh guy's finger up his arse before either.'

We never did see any photos of that day.

I didn't spill the beans about my role in the animal's antics until we were on the plane home a few days later. The funny thing was, Steve had to go home, covered in scratches and scars, and try to explain to his beloved wife that they had been made by a loveable Koala bear and not a hot Australian chick. I wish I'd been a fly on the wall when he had to explain that!

Steve still tells the tale of the Attack of the Killer Koala Bear when he speaks at functions today.

I was the only player not to get a cap in Australia. Again, I felt cheated and disappointed. What made it worse was I didn't even get to keep a jersey. In those days, they used to take the jerseys back off the reserves, if they hadn't got on the field of play. The players who actually played kept theirs, of course.

This was surely wrong. Adidas sponsored us, so it was no skin off the WRU's nose. But I didn't get any kit. I was on the bench 13 times for my country and I never got anything, not even a pair of socks or shorts. I tell people now, and they don't believe me. One of the most successful periods in Welsh rugby history and because I didn't get on the field, I didn't get a shirt. I felt like Oliver Twist in the workhouse going up and begging for another bowl of porridge,

Naturally, I tried on numerous occasions to sneak a shirt out in my kit bag, but the committee stood guarding each exit like aggressive prison wardens. They'd check everything. My kit bag, under my coat, even between the cheeks of my arse; they must had heard the ten bob note story. They would hover menacingly by the doors, as if ready for a full strip search, rubber gloves on their hands and a probe at the ready.

'Ok Watkins, pass it over. We know you have them.'

It was unbelievable. They expected players like me to give

everything and in return get bugger all. It wasn't that I couldn't keep the shirt which bothered me. The real issue was they had made a rule that the subs would under no circumstance get one. I was part of the team that had won its third Grand Slam and a third consecutive Triple Crown. I had played my part, even if I hadn't actually played, yet.

I had nothing to show anyone I was ever involved, except for a few funny stories.

# 5

# One Stray Boot and a Bottle of Beer

*"Spike the Captain — A great leader, very good knowledge of the game. A man who led by example. Spike the Player - A great hooker, excellent at throwing into the lineout, excellent striker of the ball in scrum. He was a tough nut who wouldn't take a step backwards. He was a real pleasure to play alongside. Spike the Man — Great company to be with, although he did border on the edge of madness"*

**Ian 'Ikey' Stephens**
**Bridgend - Wales - British Lions**

Not long after the Australian tour, my involvement in the Welsh squad came to an abrupt end for many years. The following November saw me arrested for the nightclub incident and banned from playing for Wales. Cardiff banned me as well. At one stage I must have been the most banned rugby player in Wales, probably the whole world. The "Adolf 'Spikey' Hitler of the Welsh Valleys", goose-stepping on to muddy fields in dirty rugby boots and a worn out gum shield.

*'The dirtiest fucker I've ever played against.'* Mike Teague, the flanker and hard man of English rugby, once said about me in

The Sunday Times. They didn't actually print the word, *fucker*, but reading between the lines, that's what he meant. 'Spikey Watkins is the dirtiest player I've ever played against.' it said it there in black and white for the whole world to see.

Someone showed it to me, and asked me how I felt about it.

'Thoroughly deserved,' I replied and cut it out for my scrap book.

By the time I had served my long ban from Cardiff, I was hungry to make up for lost time. I put my heart and soul into becoming the main man at the club once again, on and off the field. On away trips I wasn't content to be the one at the back of the bus messing about. I also wanted simultaneously to be the one at the front on the microphone. I wanted complete control. I tried my best to keep on the straight and narrow, and let my rugby do the talking.

On the field, Phillips and I still jostled for the hooker position. Even though he was by then the number one Welsh hooker, he wasn't guaranteed a place in his club side. Cardiff had the honour of playing against the New Zealand All Blacks, on their tour of the UK in 1980. I desperately wanted to play, but I didn't think in a million years I would get the nod ahead of Phillips. The week before, I'd been selected to play against Northampton and had quite a good game. Later that evening, in the club house, our coach John Ryan called me over. 'Hey Spikey, in your opinion, who are the best two props at the club?' he asked me.

I didn't have to think twice. 'Jeff Whitefoot and Ian Eidman,' I replied.

He called the two of them over. 'Hey guys, Spikey here, wants you two to be his props for next week's game against the All Blacks.' They looked at each other. I shrugged my shoulders. 'So I suggest,' he said to them both, 'you don't leave him out of your sight until the game.'

What a great piece of man-management by John. Not only did he instantly form a bond between myself and the props, he also ensured both of them did whatever was required to keep me out of any trouble. And they did. Everywhere I went, they would follow. Even to the toilet.

Ousting Phillips from the side to play New Zealand was a massive feather in my cap. Not many players get to face the world's best team. In total, I played against them twice for Cardiff, and I also played twice against the New Zealand Maoris.

I rushed home and said to my father. 'Dad, I've been picked to play against New Zealand. Here are two tickets for you and Mam to come and watch.' I stood there in the front room as proud as punch.

He looked at them, and then at me. He shook his head slowly and then ripped the two tickets up in front of me. 'Have a good game, son, but make sure the lorries are loaded by six the morning after.'

I stood there speechless. The ripped-up tickets littered the floor. I didn't know if I wanted to cry or punch him. I didn't do either. I walked out. Rugby was nothing to my father. It was all about work. I could understand that in a way. However, for God's sake, a little appreciation of his son's achievements wouldn't have gone amiss from time to time. The biggest game of my career thus far, and I had to get up and leave the Angel Hotel at 4am the next morning, battered and bruised and slightly hungover, to rush home to change into my working clothes, and be in Ebbw Vale by six, to load the lorries.

It felt as if I was fighting a war on all fronts!

I had a great time playing for Cardiff. The functions and the games, and the people I met, were unbelievable. I was there during their centenary year. I got to play at the National Stadium with the club about 12 times, before I finally ran out with Wales a few years later. The club made a great effort with my wife and kids. They always put on family events and looked after my daughters on match days. They couldn't do enough for us.

Like I mentioned before, part of the reason for playing rugby is to go on tour at the end of the season and with Cardiff I went on some corkers. One of the first was to Canada and America during the club's centenary. We went for an entire month. Once again, to leave work and the business for that long proved to be financial suicide and another nail in the coffin of the relationship between me and my old man, but at that time the trip was a once-in-a-lifetime experience. I simply couldn't miss it.

The monthly instalments for the truck, tax and insurance, plus basic household things, like bills, food and electric had to come from somewhere. If I didn't turn my wheels I didn't turn any money. That was my biggest enemy, the time and the money I lost while playing the sport I loved. Many players at Cardiff worked in banks or schools and their wages often got paid when they were away with the club. Mine didn't and right up to the day of the trip, I tried to somehow make up the money I would lose by being out of the country for so long. I worked doublers, extra hours, and all day on Sundays, just so the bills would be paid when I left.

The night after one of our matches in Canada, myself and another player went missing in action. I could have said we'd been abducted by aliens or chased by a yeti but let's just say that there may have been women involved somewhere along the line. The next morning, our bus waited and waited in Kamloops, the home of the jumping trout, to head back to Vancouver. At around that same time, my very own trout was doing some exploring of its own and simply could not be disturbed. In the end, they left us there. We had to make our own way back. The committee took a dim view of our behaviour, but forgave us quite quickly.

When I first went down to Cardiff, lots of people reckoned I wouldn't last there unless I started behaving myself. They said Cardiff wouldn't put up with me but I didn't find the club like that at all. To their credit, they weren't stuck in their ways like many clubs. Even though they were the most famous club in the world and at one stage even had three British Lions scrum halves in their squad, they still liked a bit of fun. They played hard and in the words of Gerald Davies, like to 'Parity' hard as well.

One of the reasons I liked the club so much was that to be on the Cardiff committee you had to have been an ex-player. So they knew the *craic*. I'm not a committee person as you can gather; I'm more like the anti-committee person, the 666 of committee men. So in my view, the more ex-players, or certain ex-players, involved behind the scenes the better.

But however much I liked them, it didn't stop me trying to get one over on them wherever possible. That's just the way I'm wired. On another occasion on that North American tour, me and a couple of the boys gathered in my hotel room, having a few beers and a laugh. Everybody was starving, but we didn't want to order anything to our rooms because we had to pay for it. As usual I had an idea. I phoned down to reception and ordered the works, steaks, lobster, champagne and plenty more beer. It amounted to three trolleys full of grub. I asked for it to be sent to a committee man's room, one floor below us.

'Yes, sir,' the receptionist stated, 'it will be with you in around 30 minutes.'

Twenty minutes later, three of us waited by the lift on the floor below. When the waiter appeared, I told him I was the committeeman in question. I signed the room service bill in the name of Brian Mark and then we pretended to wheel the trolleys into 'my' room.

As soon as the waiter disappeared, we sneaked the trolleys upstairs to our proper room. We had one hell of a feast. When we finished, we took the empty trolleys back down stairs and left them outside Brian's room.

No one was any the wiser.

As we waited on the bus next morning, the hotel manager came rushing on and stood at the front. 'There's a large outstanding bill for room $257,' he announced.

'Whose room is that?' A committeeman said as he stood up and eyeballed all the players one by one.

A confused Brian put his hand up. 'That's my room,' he said, 'but I didn't have any food or drink sent to my room.'

I shouted out, 'Oh see...it's alright for the committee to order stuff to their rooms but us players can't. That's not fair.'

Brian Mark proclaimed his innocence and couldn't work out how the trolleys loaded with food had been ordered, delivered, signed for, eaten and the empties left outside his room afterwards. The committee settled the bill. We gave him some ribbing for the rest of the tour. I've always stressed that tours are all about survival of the fittest and creativeness!

We spent a fabulous few days on Vancouver Island and played Crimson Tide. A young Gareth Rees, who later in life went on to play for and captain Canada told me years later, how his Dad had taken him to the game. It was that match which inspired him to take up the sport, he told me.

Probably the best and funniest trip away with Cardiff was to Zimbabwe a few years later. We played and won all our four games, beating their national side twice. But with players like Gareth Davies, Robert Norster and John Scott, I would have been disappointed if we hadn't. We had a top notch outfit, which was far too strong for many of the emerging rugby countries.

One night during the trip, Alan Phillips came over and plonked himself down next to me. He held out his hand. 'Hey Spikey, isn't it time we buried the hatchet.'

Slightly drunk, I slowly turned to face him. I looked him square in the eye and uttered, 'Yeah, I'll bury the hatchet; I'll bury it in your fucking head. Now fuck off from me.'

He huffed and puffed before stomping away. I didn't care a toss. The mere sight of him wound me up like a top.

The next day, we headed out to play the second test in Harare. I was faced with the ultimate case of Sod's Law. My rugby boots split when warming up. Trust my bloody luck because I didn't have a spare pair. What made it even worse was that the only person not playing, to have boots in my size was, you guessed it, Alan *get away from me, or I'm going to put a hatchet in your head* Phillips.

I thought I'd rather go on the field bare footed than ask him for his boots, but was told not to be so stupid and stubborn.

Through clenched teeth I sidled up to him and asked as nicely as I could. All the other players sat about listening and pissing themselves laughing.

'Of course,' he replied, then he grinned and added, 'But watch out though Spikey, they maybe too fast for you.'

'Where was that hatchet when I needed it?' I thought. As quick as a flash I returned, 'I'm more afraid of them running away from rucks and mauls.'

After the game, we all had a couple of beers. All the players were ribbing me because Phillips had lent me his boots. I could hear one of them say, 'Oh, Spikey and Alan are best buddies now.' They kept on and on. It bugged me so much that I grabbed Alan's boots, went outside and threw them as hard as I could onto the roof of the clubhouse. Phillips had to get someone to climb up on the roof to get them back.

A few hours later, we all wanted to get back to the hotel at the other end of the city so we could go out on the town. For some reason the driver refused to drive the bus. Ever the diplomat, I firmly but politely asked him again and again, but he still wouldn't budge. At this stage I may have lost my patience and yelled at him to get going. He still wouldn't move so I kept up the pressure. In the end he jumped off the bus and refused to get back on. All the Cardiff committee were up in arms again.

'What have you bloody well done now, Spikey?'

'Don't worry, I have my HGV class 1 license' I yelled as I got in the driver's seat and revved the engine. Everyone thought I was messing about. With all the boys egging me on, I put it in gear and pulled off. The committeemen didn't know what to do. If they stopped me, we wouldn't get home. If they didn't and we got stopped, all hell would break loose.

I just put my foot down and drove through the crowded city streets. All the boys cheered when I pulled up to the hotel.

Bright and early the following morning, I got summoned in front of the committee. The boys thought I would be shipped home on the next plane for 'upsetting' the driver and 'borrowing' his bus. The committee gave me a dressing down, telling me how stupid I had been and how they couldn't condone my actions. I had to promise them I wouldn't do anything like it again.

I don't know what it was with me and buses. Years later, when I played for Newport, I jumped in and hid our bus in the car park at Severn Bridge Services when the driver popped off for a quick slash. The bus company complained that I could have smashed up their new £150,000 bus and threatened to stop driving the team to away matches if I was on board.

Back to the Zimbabwe tour, and a few days later, the

committee were on maximum alert due to us having a relaxation day, but I couldn't stop myself. Someone really should have drugged me or tied me to a bed. I think I've always been the same. When I was training or playing I was fine. Very serious, very focused. It was the downtime in between games which got me in most trouble. I've been told many times that I reminded people of the rugby version of McMurphy, the character Jack Nicholson played in 'One Flew over the Cuckoo's Nest', but maybe with a lot more testosterone.

I decided I would behave and not do anything stupid. So while most of the boys lay up on the roof of the hotel, sun bathing or swimming in the pool, I went for a walk by myself. My goal of not doing anything "stupid" didn't last long. Just outside the hotel, I spotted a guy selling pots, plates and stuff off the back of two donkeys, one big one and a smaller, younger version. I assumed it was a mother donkey and it's young. Looking at all the crappy tourist gifts strapped to their backs, a bout of wickedness engulfed me. I hatched a plan.

'Hey mate, can I hire the small donkey?' I asked the guy.

He didn't understand.

Speaking slowly in Pidgin English, and making hand signals I tried to explain I would give him money if I could borrow his animal for an hour. I didn't know exactly what I wanted to do with it; I just knew it would be fun. The owner kept refusing, until I gave him a hard dig in the ribs. No, I didn't. I didn't go round the world digging people in the ribs, honest, well unless they were playing rugby against me. He eventually agreed when I gave him all the money in my pocket.

Chuffed, I led the animal away. It must have taken one look at me, and thought; 'Now I'm in bloody trouble.'

'I know,' I thought, 'I'll show the boys my new pet.' I led the donkey up the steps at the front of the hotel, through the lobby towards the lift. The girl on reception had no chance of stopping me. The poor mule kept slipping and sliding on the polished marble floor. Suddenly, it stopped dead and wouldn't budge. I pulled and pushed. It was a stubborn young thing, and a right strong little bleeder, I don't mind telling you.

The girl on reception was going mental. She shouted at me and waved her arms about. I ignored her and dragged the donkey across the floor. It must have looked like some kind of bizarre Disney film.

I finally got the thing into the lift and pushed the button for the top floor. As we travelled up, with the background music playing, it reminded me of that sketch with Peter Sellers, when they were all in the lift and one of them farted. I looked at the donkey, 'I'm blaming you,' I laughed to myself.

At the top, the lift doors opened. Walking out into the bright sunlight, I slapped the animal on the arse and let it go. People screamed. Waiters carrying trays ran for cover. One waiter fell back and ended up in the swimming pool. The donkey raced about aimlessly. It too ended up in the pool. I jumped in to rescue it. Some of the other boys did the same. There was donkey poo everywhere. Chaos ensued as we tried to pull the creature to safety. God knows what would have happened if there hadn't been a walk-in shallow end. I can only begin to imagine the headlines in the Western Mail. 'Mental Rugby Player Drowns Donkey'.

I would have been banned for life everywhere if I had drowned the bloody thing. Eventually, we dragged the frightened animal out. I realise it was bordering on animal cruelty. But I didn't mean any harm; like I said I was bored and needed something to do.

I eventually got it back in the lift. Tip-toed it back through reception and gave it back, in one piece just about, to its owner.

There was murder the next day. The hotel management went mental. I thought I was going home for sure. But again, the powers-that-be at Cardiff eventually saw the funny side of it.

Back on the rugby front, the following season I kept plugging away for Cardiff and I was selected to play for Wales B for the third time, against the French once again but this time on their own turf.

I didn't know what to think. My friends, my family, and even my bloody postman warned me that it was my last chance.

'Just go and play your game, Spikey,' Terry lectured me after training one night. 'Don't do anything stupid.'

'I didn't want him to tell me that,' I thought, he's cursed me now. Something was bound to go tits-up. And just as if my worst enemy had scripted it, it did.

This time I'm adamant it wasn't entirely my fault. It started off badly, and got gradually worse. For some reason the Welsh newspapers printed an article about me, with the headline, *The Man of Steel on his way to France.* I didn't know why. Other than delivering stuff to steel works it didn't really mean anything. But just try telling that to the French. I envisaged the big, ugly, French bastards, who had been fed raw meat all week, rubbing their hairy hands together and sharpening their studs when they were told that. I know what my team talk would have been if the boot had been on the other foot! 'If this man of steel from France doesn't get carried off in the first five minutes, you're going off.' I would have told my pack.

On the day I may as well have had a 'mod' target painted on my forehead.

At the very first scrum, their second row, whose mother must have trapped his head in a car door when he was a kid, punched me square on the side of my head. Stars appeared in front of my eyes. 'I hope it's not going to be like this all game' I thought.

Next scrum, more or less the same. That was it. I knew I

had to do something, or I was going to get carried off, and I definitely wasn't going to get carried off.

I waited for my opportunity. Then by a giant stroke of luck, at the very next ruck, their big second row's head popped out on our side. He growled up at me from the ground. Without thinking twice about it, I booted him right in the chops. A full toe-poke in the face. Did I regret it? No way. Minutes earlier he had been using me as a human punch bag. As the old saying goes, 'if you live by the sword, you die by the sword', and his sword that night came in the shape of my size nine rugby boots.

The noise of the kick reverberated around the mountains. A big Oohhhhh escaped from the crowd. All the other French players piled in to me.

When order was finally restored, they carted him off dazed, his nose badly broken. In my mind, I could hear a bell ringing and people chanting, 'Bring out your dead.'

Well, he started it. I didn't go looking for it.

After the game, one of the WRU committeemen marched up to me. 'That was the dirtiest thing I have ever seen on a rugby field in my life.'

'Was it now?' I piped at him, 'Pity you hadn't been in my boots when he was punching my head in at every scrum. He was trying to knock my head off.'

'But there was still no need for that. It will be the happiest day of my life when you are not playing for Wales,' he added.

'Up yours!' I grunted and walked away. It made me sick how these men, on the safety of the touchline, thought they could tell me what I should and shouldn't have done.

Next came the icing on my cake. Later that evening, after a few beers, a gang of us walked from the reception towards the town. The boys were playing about with a beer bottle, passing it about like a rugby ball.

'Don't mess about now boys.' I took it off them and innocently chucked it across the road, but it smashed against a wall. I know it was a stupid thing to do, but I didn't mean it to smash. I was just trying to be the good guy for once.

Another selector, standing up on the balcony, saw me throwing the bottle. Conveniently he hadn't seen me take it off the boys in the first place.

The bottle incident sealed my fate. Unfairly, my name got put in the big black book yet again. This time I had been trying to stop the problem, but again I was the one who ended up in trouble. I'm positive certain members of the committee wanted me to do stupid things so they could throw the book at me. They didn't want me in the team. Some of the stuffy-nosed ones didn't understand me at all.

One selector said, when we travelled to the airport, 'Spikey, you have burnt your boots this time. You will never represent Wales in any form ever again.'

There seemed to be a recurring and negative theme to these conversations.

Even some of the other players moved away from me at the airport. I don't think they wanted to be associated with my actions by default. I felt cursed, like I had the plague. I came home from France feeling like a convict just released from jail.

Not for the first time, I went from being on the inside looking out, to being so far on the outside I couldn't see where the bloody inside was, even with a pair of binoculars.

I thought about packing it all in, walking away and doing something else. I needed a new challenge in my life.....then I had a call from a good old friend.

# 6

# Charlie Faulkner RFC

*"I always said that Spikey was like a rubber ball....whatever people threw at him....he just kept bouncing back. I also reckoned when he was on form (which was most of the time) Spikey could tell what colour socks someone had on even if they were wearing Wellington boots."*

**Charlie Faulkner**
**Pontypool - Wales - British Lions**

Although the record books show I played and captained Newport for four seasons from 1983 to 1987, in fact, as far as I was concerned I never ever actually played for them.

Alright, I did, but in my mind, I didn't. Confused? Well, let me explain. I disliked Newport with a passion, always have and probably always will. Not the supporters mind you. They were great to me. It was just the committee I couldn't take to.

Up to 1981 I was still playing for Cardiff. Although I was getting lots of game time, to a degree I felt I was being treated unfairly. I was the one getting picked to play in all the hard games. The likes of Neath away, Swansea away, Llanelli away, Bridgend and Pontypool. While Phillips, who was the Wales hooker, played in what I would class as all the 'easier' fixtures

My father in Burma, during the Second World War.

My Mam, my Dad and me at Cathryn's christening in Cwmcarn.

The young Michael John Watkins. Here I am at about 18 months old.

The teenage Spikey in Spain, on my
first-ever holiday abroad.

Playing for Cwmcarn Youth. Not
sure if I'm going to throw the ball
in or lump someone!!

Happy days at Crumlin RFC. A few of those guys are no longer with us, RIP.

Paul Turner, MJ Watkins and Steve Cheshire. A photo that hangs in Crumlin RFC, where we all started playing rugby.

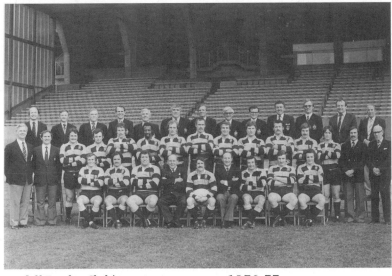

Cardiff Rugby Club's centenary season 1976-77.

Playing for Cardiff against Aberavon. I am just about to run at the late Clive Shell. A very young Terry Holmes in the background and my old mate Robbo are also pictured.

My darling daughters come to meet me straight from school after Cardiff's tour to Zimbabwe 1981. Happy days.

Doing a bit of cleaning at Heathrow Airport before departing for Cardiff's centenary tour to Canada and America.

Playing against British Columbia in Vancouver on the centenary tour. In the photo along with me, is Gerry Wallace, Robbo, Carl Smith and Roger Lane.

## PROBABLES

J. P. R. Williams (Bridgend)
T. G. R. Davies (Cardiff)
R. Gravell (Llanelli)
S. P. Fenwick (Bridgend)
J. J. Williams (Llanelli)
P. Bennett (Llanelli)
G. O. Edwards (Cardiff)
A. G. Faulkner (Pontypool)
R. W. Windsor (Pontypool)
G. Price (Pontypool)
G. A. D. Wheel (Swansea)
A. J. Martin (Aberavon)
T. J. Cobner (Pontypool, capt.)
D. P. Quinnell (Llanelli)
T. P. Evans (Swansea)

## POSSIBLES

W. Davies (Neath)
E. Rees (Neath)
R. Bergiers (Llanelli)
D. Burcher (Newport)
B. Juliff (Pontypridd)
J. Bevan (Aberavon, capt.)
C. Shell (Aberavon)
G. Shaw (Neath)
M. Watkins (Cardiff)
J. Richardson (Aberavon)
R. Thomas (London Welsh)
C. Davis (Newbridge)
C. Burgess (Ebbw Vale)
J. Squire (Newport)
T. David (Pontypridd)

Replacements: C. Griffiths (Llanelli), G. Evans (Newport), C. Rees (London Welsh), D. Richards (Swansea), B. Williams (Cardiff), C. Williams (Aberavon), W. James (Aberavon), P. May (Llanelli), D. Church (Cross Keys).

Kick-off 2.15 p.m.

The WRU Trial Match. Probables v. Possibles, held on Saturday 1st January 1977 at Cardiff Arms Park. It was a full-blown match with battles for every position. The Probables won 6-3.

The Welsh squad who toured Australia 1978. Packed full of established Welsh legends and the 'new kids on the block'.

In honour of those Welshmen who have brought to Wales the first Treble Crown and a new record of 8 " Grand Slams "

I anrhydeddu'r Cymry glew a sicrhaodd i Gymru y Goron Driphlyg deirgwaith yn olynol am y tro cyntaf, a record newydd o wyth Camp Lawn

The Prime Minister
and Mrs. James Callaghan

request the honour of the company of

Mr and Mrs M Watkins

at a Reception at 10 Downing Street, Whitehall
on Monday, 3rd April, 1978, from 6.00 p.m. to 7.30 p.m.

*An answer is requested to :*
The Secretary (Invitations)
10 Downing Street, Whitehall

Another proud moment. The invitation to 10 Downing Street in April 1978 to celebrate our achievements.

With the Wales squad in London before the summer tour to Australia in 1978.

at that time such as the Harlequins and the Coventrys of this world.

I came to the conclusion I was helping my biggest rival out. He was having an easy ride, shining in all the easier fixtures where they would win scoring lots of points into the bargain. I'd had enough. I wanted to expose him for the overrated player I believed he was. The only way to do that was to play against him, and prove I could do it whoever I played for.

Although I was being selected for many of the big games, I still wasn't guaranteed regular first team action. I wanted to stay and fight for my place, but I also felt my game would benefit from being able to play regularly, and it would put me back in the spotlight.

While my Cardiff future hung in the balance, Ray Gravell, the captain of Llanelli, knocked on my door. I had huge respect for Ray, a true gentleman and a Scarlet through and through. He asked me if I would be interested in heading west and playing for them. One night, I met him and a posse of committeemen in the Bear Hotel in Cowbridge. They offered me the vice-captaincy to join them.

Their proposition took me completely by surprise. I was so tempted. The only issue I had was my work. As a self-employed lorry driver the job still took me all over the country. I didn't know where I would be from one day to the next. I had a difficult enough time getting back to Gwent or Cardiff for training, let alone driving another hour and a half to Llanelli. On saying that, I did think long and hard about it. I would have loved to have played for them. Their brand of running rugby would have suited my all-action style of play, and with Ray's fire-breathing passion I believe I would have fitted in quite well.

In the end, strictly down to work commitments, I had to tell Ray I couldn't do it. He understood, and never held it against me.

In 1981, Charlie had retired from playing rugby. No one knew how old he was. Some jokingly said he must have been about 70 when we toured Australia years before. Anyway, he took over the coaching role at a very unorganised and badly-led Newport. The club was at an all time low. Everyone had baled out on the place. No one wanted to be there. From the outset it appeared to be a complete hell hole. They had lost something like 21 games on the trot. In many quarters, they were regarded as a worse team than Penarth; and Penarth were just above pond life.

Charlie, a Newport boy from Pill, wanted to do his best to help the club. He called me up and asked me to pop down the house for a 'chat'. We sat in his front room as he shouted to his wife Gill to make us some tea and bring in the posh biscuits.

'You know why I'm talking to you don't you,' he said, sat there in his cardigan.

'Yeah I know.'

'Well.'

'Well what Charl?' I loved winding him up.

'You know what.'

'What?'

'You know what. How do you fancy coming to play for Newport, you idiot?'

'No Charlie,' I was straight with my reply, 'I can't stand the place. As a matter of fact, to start with, I hate the colour of the jerseys.'

I could see his mind ticking over, wondering if he had the authority to change the colour of the kit. We sat and drank our tea. He pleaded with me a few more times, but got the same response.

Finally, he shrugged. 'Well, I gave it a go,' he said, 'I gave it my best shot, didn't I?'

I'd made my mind up. I really didn't want to go there. It had been well documented that Newport were in the doldrums and was an unhappy place to be. As we walked down the path he turned, 'Hang on, I will give it one more shot. How about if you don't come and play for Newport.'

'Charlie, you've been eating too many bloody digestives.'

'No! Look, don't come and play for Newport. Come and play for me?'

I looked straight at him. I loved Charlie to bits. I would do anything for the man. I made a decision right there on the spot. 'Ok, I will come and play for you but I will never play for Newport. How's that?'

We shook on it, right there in his garden. And that's how I came to play for Charlie Faulkner RFC and not Newport.

'Can we change the colour of the jerseys?' I joked.

'Too late now Spikey, its all water under the river.' He had a habit of mixing his metaphors up.

Newport had only won 19 out of 48 games the previous season, with many of their losses by big margins to their biggest rivals. Before Charlie came on board they struggled to raise two sides for a pre-season trial.

People told me I was mad to leave Cardiff, the Schweppes Cup holders, to go to a club who had been knocked out in the first round. Everyone warned me about Newport, and what they were like. Terry Holmes and the rest of the Cardiff crowd begged me not to go there. They said by going there I would be kissing goodbye to my international future. With what I had been told by different members of the WRU, I thought I had more chance of being the bodyguard to the Queen than playing for Wales again so that didn't bother me.

Although I didn't have faith in the committee at Newport, I did have faith and belief in Charlie. Stepping across that line cemented us as lifelong friends. He never once let me down, and I tried my best to do the same for him. He also pushed my case to play for Wales at every opportunity.

So in the 1982/3 season I left the fashionable city club to go and play for the unfashionable side near the border. I had been with Cardiff for seven seasons and enjoyed most of it. What I did appreciate and what really touched me was that the Cardiff committee were the first to send a letter of congratulations when I captained Wales and won my first cap. The letter said, 'Glad things have worked out for you in the end and you have had your just rewards.' A very classy touch I thought, even though by then I was playing for their biggest rivals.

At Newport, Charlie and I brought in the former Cardiff and Monmouthshire player and Bedwas captain, Roy Duggan, as assistant coach and backs coach. Roy was a great guy and remains a mate of mine to this day.

My playing career at the Black and Ambers didn't start too well. In only my second game I got sent off playing at Blackheath, for stamping on someone's head. The maddening thing was I got dismissed by the chairman of Blackheath, after the original ref got injured and he took over. Apparently, he had seen me doing things he didn't like from the touchline. I got banned for four weeks

'Sorry Charl....I let you down,' I told him later that night.

'You haven't let me down at all, Spikey my boy, not at all.'

The rest of my first season went reasonably well. I played 50 games out of a total of 54, the first time anyone at Newport had reached a half century in one season. I also captained the side 17 times and won the Supporters' Player of the Year. More importantly, I think I had done my little bit, along with Charlie, to help the revival of Newport after four disastrous years.

From that initial season, I especially remember my first Newport v Cardiff game at the Arms Park. Sadly, but not surprisingly, Phillips cried off at the last minute. Better to cry off, than get carried off I guess. In the words of the famous ex-Manchester United footballer, Roy Keane, 'I would wait for my opportunity.'

Phillips or no Phillips, I still wanted to show my old team mates what they were missing. At their first lineout, I glared across at my old mate Terry Holmes, playing scrum-half.

'I'm having you Terry, boy,' I warned him.

He looked at me, grinned and simply said, 'Michael John.' He always called me that, especially on the occasions when the red mist came down on the field and my head went. He knew that those two words would bring me back to normality. Whilst others in the team would be yelling, 'Stop Spikey' or 'Cool it' or 'come on now', Terry would simply whisper, 'Michael John, cool down.'

In return I always called him Terence David, if he ever lost it.

So while I was getting ready to race around the lineout and smash him to bits, he simply said, 'Michael John, have you seen yourself in that jersey? You look like a fucking bumble bee.' His words deflated me. I knew I should have made Charlie change the bloody colour of the shirts before I signed. Terry kept mocking me all game. And I never got close enough to lay a hand on him.

During my second season I got voted club captain. I was more than chuffed because I knew the players, the committee and the fans wanted me to lead them. It was a big honour. I became totally immersed in my new role. I liked being in the position of making the decisions, even if they were the wrong ones at times. I had always classed myself a winner when playing sport. Many people have told me they believed I was born to hook and to lead. With my competitive, in-your-face, inspirational style and leadership, I think I brought the best out of our pack of forwards.

Charlie became a massive inspiration both on and off the field. As an ex-prop, he was a marvellous help because he knew all the tricks of front row play. He used to call me the Muhammad Ali of his pack but I never knew exactly what he meant. Was I a good player, a good talker like the famous boxer or was it that I could fight like him, or all three? I never asked him and he never told me.

Charlie and I were like-minded in our attitude to the game. It had to be hard, uncompromising and we adopted a no-frills approach, building our vision on the solid foundation of a formidable forward unit that didn't take a step backwards. We created a team within a team. The standard of Newport's forward play improved dramatically, hopefully reflecting the work we both put in. Not only could we finally look rival packs in the eyes, we could also blacken them if they wanted trouble! We got the boys playing on the edge. It wasn't pretty, but sometimes in life you have to do, what you have to do.

I began to thoroughly enjoy playing for Charlie Faulkner RFC and not for one moment did I regret having made the move. While Newport helped me in so many ways, I also helped put them back on their feet and regain some long overdue respect.

On a deadly serious note, one thing I did change was the outrageous initiation ceremony players carried out on any new member. In my opinion, it bordered on sexual assualt. I'd heard that certain members of the club, well thought of members, gave new players blow jobs in the initiation ceremony. Now, no one would ever accuse me of being a killjoy, but there is a line that not even I would cross. I was always up for a *craic*, but what they were doing in Newport just wasn't acceptable.

The stories I heard were better suited to an extreme porn film, not a rugby club, so when I got made captain I stopped it all. I stopped all the nonsense of tying boys up, and whipping them with wet towels and worse. It wasn't a laugh, just an excuse to bully and sexually humiliate people. How could they ever expect to attract good, young, players from places like nearby universities when all that was going on? Those talented young players didn't want to come and who could blame them. Who would want to get the shit beaten out of them and then get fondled by a bunch of senior players? We continued having an initiation ceremony; that's a part of the fabric of any rugby club. But it consisted of drinking games and playful things like that, nothing more.

I remember in my first year going on a trip to Vancouver in Canada with the club. I was about 29 at that time. Charlie took me to one side, 'you have to go through your initiation today Spikey....What you going to do?'

'I ain't going to do anything Charl' I said. In my mind I didn't play for Newport, I played for Charlie.

'You will have to go through it, though' he reiterated.

'Ok, of course I will, don't worry.'

I could tell he was worried, and probably for good reason. I warned them all if there was any funny business I would murder someone. They tied me up and put two pillow cases over my head. I couldn't see anything. They led me into a room. I could hear them all sniggering in the background. Someone shoved some deep heat up my arse. They started pushing me around, calling me names and swearing at me. Then the punching and kicking rained in on me. Because I had played for Cardiff there was a bit more aggression to their attack. They asked me lots of questions, but I wouldn't answer them. I kept telling myself that I was stronger than them and I knew the pillow cases were going to come off at some stage. What they didn't appreciate was that once upset, I was ten times worse than Zazuum, the donkey from the Arabian Nights, and they had just pulled my tail!

Still tied up and blindfolded, they sat me in a bath of ice. After they pulled me out, one bastard really dug me with a vicious punch in my ribs. It was a brutal blow meant to hurt me. I stayed on my feet and still refused to answer any of their questions.

In the end, they took the pillow cases off. My eyes bulged like saucers and inside, my anger was bubbling fast to the surface.

*'Honey, I'm home.'* I felt like the crazy husband in 'The Shining.' I glared at each and every one of them but not one of them would look me in the eye.

'Come on Spike, it's only a bit of fun. Help us with the others,' someone said.

'Hang on a second,' I thought, 'I'm in the same team as these people. Where are they coming from? "It's only a bit of fun" but for who?'

I decided to let it drop. I didn't speak. I just moved out of the way. Charlie came and sat down by me. I didn't want anything to do with it. I watched as they put the others through the bullying mill. One big bastard was digging them all hard in the ribs. I knew he was the one that had hit me.

Later that night, after a few beers, I sat there, mulling the earlier events around in my head. Charlie could sense I wasn't right. He whispered, 'Hang on now psycho....forget it. There was nothing to it. It was a bit of fun.'

But I couldn't forget it. I sat there, glaring at the bastard who had punched me. He sat, avoiding my stare, laughing and joking with the others.

'Oh, to hell with it.' Something inside me needed to be released. I walked across and punched him on the side of the head. A right beauty it was. He collapsed off his chair onto the floor. 'Come on,' I yelled, 'I'm not tied up now. Let's beat fuck out of each other now....is it? That's what you do...isn't it. Come on,' I stood above him screaming.

'Oh you're nuts,' he yelled.

Charlie led me away. But I had made my point. Having fun was having fun. Bullying wasn't fun. I stopped it all. I didn't want that type of 'fun' in my club. I wanted college boys to come and play for us. What they didn't understand was no one wanted to go and play for them, and that was one of the reasons. I only went there because of Charlie. Paul Turner said he only went there because of me. Things needed to change.

With that nonsense out of my system, we finally moved on. But it wasn't all doom and gloom and sucking boys off. I had some good times on and off the field over the years with Charlie Faulkner RFC.

One time, Naas Botha, the famous South African outside half, came to stay for a while with Brian Jones, the chairman of Newport who lived right next door to me in Cwmcarn. One evening Naas asked me if he could come training with the club, just to have a run about.

'Yeah, no problem.' I said.

When we got to the ground, all the boys stood around in awe of the Springbok legend.

'Spikey....that's Naas Botha isn't it?' someone asked me.

'Yeah, yeah.'

Charlie turned up late, with his bag of balls over his shoulder. He didn't know Naas Botha from Adam Ant.

'Who's that new bloke, Spike?

'Ask him yourself.'

He ambled across, 'What's your name son?'

'NAAS.' He pronounced it Noz.

Charlie nodded his head and ambled back. 'That's a funny name Spike...isn't it...NOZ....what kind of name is that?'

'He's from Blaenavon, Charl. You know what they're like up there.'

91

'Oh yeah, they talk like that up there don't they!'

I was dying to laugh. I told Naas not to say anything and just play along.

We started warming up. Charlie did his usual, 'How many players are here?'

I said, 'You're the coach, count them.'

'You are no help at all are you, Spike?' He started counting. The boys ran about on purpose. 'Oh, come on boys and stand still.' In the end, he just guessed. 'Right then...there's 30 here.... so I want you to split into 5 groups of 5.'

Everyone burst out laughing. I thought 'what the hell is Naas going to make of all this?' You couldn't make it up.

'What about the other five, Charl?' I asked.

'What five? Oh I don't know, they can tag along behind.'

At the end of the session, Naas took a few balls and started booting them from one end of the field to the other. Charl came up to me, out of breath. 'Bloody hell Spike...that boy can't half welly that thing. I think we may have unearthed a diamond here, Spikey boy.' He clapped his hands in joy.

'Charl, its Naas, Naas Botha.'

'I know, I know it's Noz...he's from Blaenavon.'

'No Charl. He's from South Africa. He plays outside half for the Springboks.'

Everyone burst out laughing. I could see his mind calculating what I'd told him. He huffed, 'I knew, I knew that,' he replied as he stormed off.

He didn't have a clue.

One of the highlights playing for Charlie Faulkner RFC was the day I led out the team for the Cup Final against Cardiff and when I finally came face-to-face, as it were, with my oldest enemy, Alan Phillips. A man, who in my eyes, had stolen 19 of my Welsh caps.

After pulling the club up by its bootlaces, Charlie and I finally made them good enough to get to their first cup final for donkey's years. We had no real stars like the other clubs. None of us played for Wales and we were still considered unfashionable, but I quite liked that.

The build up to the game within the media focused more on the dislike between me and Phillips than on the rivalry concerning two of Wales' greatest clubs. It came to a showdown between the two hookers. The newspaper compared us to arm wrestlers locked in a dual of strength across a table.

In my days playing for Cardiff, we had some right personal battles, but I knew this was the one that mattered. I didn't like Phillips and was more than happy to tell everyone that I didn't like him and why. But I knew I couldn't just get drawn into a personal battle. I didn't want my team's effort submerged by my private issue, and Newport against Cardiff games were normally tense affairs anyway, whatever the circumstances.

Cardiff had been in five finals in the previous six years. They were strong favourites. The Cardiff backs on their day could be outstanding, with Mark Ring, Mike Rayer and Alan Donovan. No one gave us a chance, and what's more no one gave us the credit we deserved. We'd had a very good season so far and had won the Snelling Sevens at the start of the campaign. Our objective all year had been to win the cup.

To walk onto the field in a Cup Final in front of 50,000 fans is a huge moment in anyone's career, but to also lead the team out, and see the joy on the fans' faces, was so special. I wanted it for Charlie more than anything else. It had been a long hard slog, and he had taken lots of stick.

I knew I had to control my emotions from the start. But that was easier said than done. I knew Phillips wouldn't go looking for confrontation between us, but I knew, and he knew, that I definitely would, so I used that to my advantage. I knew I had to bide my time and it would be no good going straight in there swinging like a banshee or I would get sent off and let everyone down.

I told myself to keep cool. Charlie told me to keep cool. My friends and family told me to keep cool. Even my bloody postman told me to keep cool. So I tried my best to keep cool. I kept saying all week, 'it's for the good of the team. We are going to win the Cup. Don't lose it.'

Within three minutes of the kick-off came the first scrum. The ref got us ready to pack down. I kept thinking, 'Keep cool, Spikey, remember the team, remember Charlie, remember my family, remember my friends, remember the bloody postman.' I kept cool...I kept cool...I did, well, until the very second the both packs collided, and then I butted Phillips as hard as I could. Both front rows shot up. I stared at him.

He didn't do anything. He didn't even look at me, just moaned to the ref.

First points to me.

Now I decided to wait. I didn't have to wait long. Twenty minutes later, I saw him on the floor, on the wrong side; trapped, on my side. The ball was near his head. Honest ref! Well, ok it was about six feet away, but still close enough for me to kick out at it. Of course I missed the ball by a mile and caught Phillips right in the swede. He screamed and rolled around in agony, a huge gash in his head which required 15 stitches. I had waited six years to do that.

A grin lit up my face as they carried him off. I had done him in front of 50,000 thousand people, and a referee, without getting caught.

When Phillips went off, Robert Norster grabbed me and called me a dirty so-and-so. I normally got on very well with the big second row. The next scrum I slipped my hand from around my prop's head. Norster thought I was going to whack him. Instead I just stroked him on his face. He leapt up and it all kicked off again.

'Rob,' I smirked, 'I thought you liked me more than him.'

'Fuck off you idiot.' Shouted Norster.

The game settled down after all the excitement. With Paul Turner, our outside half, having a stormer, we pushed Cardiff to the edge. Alas, in the end they just pipped us to the post, winning 28 to 21. I was gutted. We all were. I walked into the club house later, and saw Phillips sitting there with his head bandaged-up, holding his winner's medal. I wanted to whack him again, only harder and then ram it up his arse. We didn't acknowledge each other.

The following year we had a better team but again lost to Cardiff in the quarter finals after the ref bottled it. We camped on their line for 20 minutes. There had been 13 collapsed scrums and he refused to award us a penalty try.

Before each match I was always thinking of ways to wind my pack up. One night before a Newport versus Swansea game, the BBC interviewed a young Swansea kid, just out of their youth team. Richard Webster had been making quite a name for himself since stepping up to first-class rugby. The reporter asked him if he found the transition from youth to senior rugby any harder or more physical.

He said something like, 'Not really. I found youth rugby just as hard.'

I clapped my hands. That's my team talk for tomorrow sorted, I said to myself. In the changing rooms next day, I strolled in, shaking my head as I threw my bag on the floor. I really should have been an actor. 'Did you see him on the telly last night?'

Players like Roger Powell, who had played over 400 games for the club, and Glen George sat in the corner tearing the heads off babies.

'Who?' Roger grunted.

'That upstart from Swansea, that Webster kid.'

'No, no. Why?'

I puffed out my cheeks for maximum effect. I pointed to Roger, 'He said you were shit....and you.' motioning to Glen.

'What...he didn't?'

'Well, more or less he said it...shit.....all of the Newport forwards are shit.' I could see Roger's eyes rolling about in their sockets. 'Yeah, he also said senior rugby was easier than schoolboy rugby.' I turned to them. 'I'm telling you now...if he's not off the field by halftime.....you lot will be.' I sniggered to myself.

'Did he really say that?'

'I'm telling you now, that's what he said.' I pointed to Dai Waters, 'and I won't tell you all what he said about you. It will wind you up too much.'

I could see the steam coming out of their ears. I felt a bit sorry for Webster. No I didn't. He was a cheeky little runt and deserved a good, proper introduction to senior rugby. To be fair to the kid, he didn't know what hit him. Within five minutes, he was laid flat out on the turf, holding his jaw. I ambled over to him. The crowd thought I was showing concern. I kneeled down by him and whispered in his ear, 'Is this easier than schoolboy rugby, son?' He looked up at me, his nose bleeding. 'You may as well go off now boy or you are going to get carried off?'

He told me to take a running jump. He had some balls, mind. He went down about five times altogether in that first half. Yet, to give the kid credit he stayed on for all the game. He was up and down like a jack-in-the-box. My pack hit him with everything they had, and he was still there standing.

When he walked in the club house after the game, I went over to him. He took one look at me and said, 'Ok, before you say it, it is a lot harder than youth rugby.'

I shook my head, 'No, I was going to ask you what you wanted to drink?'

He was a good kid, who turned out to be good rugby player and one tough old cookie. He went on to play for Wales, went on a Lions tour and then went to play Rugby League. I don't need to say any more.

But it wasn't just the opposition we shook up. Stuart Barnes, the English International and now Sky commentator played for our club in his early days.

During one training session Stuart, playing at outside half, kept knocking the ball on and missing his kicks to touch. At half time, Charlie decided to put him in as hooker for a few scrums to teach him what it was like being a forward doing all the hard graft, while some fancy, chocolate coated, outside half messed it up all the time.

At the first scrum, I slipped my binding and gave him a few light-hearted whacks. I kept putting my hand over his eyes and nibbling on his ear. He screamed out more in shock than pain. Colin Smart and Rhys Morgan, the props, also roughed him up a little bit, but nothing too serious. Fair play to Stuart, he took it all. After a few more scrums Charlie told him to get back to outside half and stop making mistakes. It had the desired effect because Stuart didn't knock the ball on, and didn't miss a single kick to touch for the rest of the session. He even wrote about his one and only time in the front row in his own autobiography.

Two other games I played at Newport, particularly stuck in my memory.

Newport against Bristol was always classed as a local derby. All local derbies can be quite tasty, and when you add the England versus Wales element, it took the tastiness up to Chicken Vindaloo levels.

The Memorial Ground in Bristol was packed to the rafters

with over ten thousand supporters and highlights of the game were being televised the next day. It was lucky for all concerned it wasn't shown live.

The first couple of scrums had the usual bag full of dirty tricks. There was lots of sledging between players, a few flying fists and the odd stamp or three. The Bristol pack kept turning the scrum, which was very dangerous.

I called my boys in, 'Right boys, any more of that and they're having it.'

Next scrum, they did the same and it kicked off, big time. Players rolled about on the ground, whacking each other senseless. Mini battles took place all over the field. It was more like an ice-hockey game than a rugby match. The ref stood, in shock, in the middle of the pitch blowing his whistle but no one took any notice. I was rolling about on the grass with my opposite number, both punching lumps out of each other. Suddenly, I looked across and saw the referee, Inspector George Crawford, walking off. He barged past some Bristol officials, who were trying to stop him, and headed off down the tunnel.

The whole scene reminded me of an old Wild West movie where all the cowboys are fighting in the bar. Suddenly the swing doors open up and in strolls the sheriff and everyone stops. But our sheriff hadn't strolled in carrying his pistols; he'd stormed off holding his whistle.

As he disappeared out of sight, everyone stopped punching, biting and kicking each other. It was so funny because now he had gone; no one saw much point in fighting anymore.

I turned to the guy I was hitting and said, 'Where the fuck is he going?' When the incident was shown on the television news later that night, you could see me mouthing those words. My mother called me up straight away and said, 'Michael your language is disgusting!'

Back on the field I thought, 'we better do something about this. There's a big crowd here and the television cameras. This isn't good.' So I raced after the ref and the Bristol captain, Nigel Pomphrey came rushing after me.

'Nigel,' I whispered, 'we need to sort this out otherwise there's going to be repercussions. We need to get him to restart the game.'

We both raced down the tunnel. I knocked on the ref's door. There was no reply. I kept knocking. Nothing.

'Maybe he's topping himself.'

'Maybe he's gone.'

With a little trepidation I poked my head around the door. 'Ref...Ref...are you here?'

He was stood in the shower, ranting about violence and having no control and other gibberish. He seemed to have completely lost the plot.

'Look ref,' I said, 'we've got to get the game started again. Lets just say you were took short, needed a shit....and came off.'

Ok, I agree now, it had been the wrong thing to say at that moment but I didn't know what else to do. He wasn't having any of it. He stood there with a towel around him, shaking, and pointing yet with no words coming out of his mouth. He finally told us to leave and he started to get dressed.

I was conscious there were still players out on the field, a large crowd getting more and more restless and that the cameras were still filming. When we came out of the changing room, I said to Nigel, 'Look Nigel, Bristol and Newport have been playing each other for over 100 years. This could turn into a big issue.' I added, 'I will promise you now, I will not blame Bristol, if you promise not to blame Newport.'

We shook hands on it and showing some kind of rugby camaraderie we walked back out into the spotlight. Surrounded by TV and press we both blamed the ref and said he had the shits. No, I didn't, but I should have. I said he had simply lost control. And he had. I know we were fighting, but he was supposed to have been equipped to handle that.

The game continued when a replacement ref was found. I did mention to Nigel maybe Charlie could take control. But he declined.

The story became headline news the world over. The first ever referee to walk off in protest about gratuitous violence on the pitch. Later, our runaway ref, Inspector Crawford, was issued with a severe reprimand by the powers-that-be and I don't think he ever took control of a match again.

With the incident at Bristol still on everyone's lips, I thought a friendly game against the touring Fijian rugby team, a week later, would help us to show the world we weren't the thugs some were making us out to be.

How wrong could I have been? It should have been a showpiece game and the highlight of our season with over 8,000 fans packed into Rodney Parade to see some South Sea sparkle. What they didn't expect was rugby's version of World War Three.

Before the game started, I was worried about them running us ragged. In hindsight, I should have been more concerned about them kicking us to pieces. We had heard stories that they had been to Australia and had been quite aggressive but I didn't think anything of it. I knew how the Aussies loved to moan.

From the start, there was a bit of niggling. Then it all kicked off, when the Fijian second row, Ilaitia Savai, head-butted our centre, Paul Daniels (and no, it wasn't bloody magic!!). He flattened him, knocking him out cold. I honestly thought he'd killed him. Savai got his marching order, and later got banned for six weeks.

I called all my players to arms. 'We ain't having this. Let's show them what we're made of.'

From the restart, a horrendous punch-up broke out. It was like a street brawl. It made the scrap in Bristol look like line-dancing. If Crawford had been refereeing his head would have exploded. The *fracas* lasted a good five minutes. Everyone was at it. I'm sure the guy selling hot dogs got involved at one point. One of their players ran in and karate-kicked me in the chest, Hong Kong Phooey-style. It was a free-for-all, a full-on bloodbath which continued right through the game. We lost the game by a point but no one remembered the score line. The changing rooms afterwards looked like an A&E department. Everyone had cuts and bruises and black eyes. After the game I said that they were the most illegal side in world rugby and I believe the Police were asked to investigate the match. The WRU feared the same thing would happen when Wales played them a week later but maybe we had softened them up, because the international game passed off without incident.

They say everything comes in threes. Well, a few weeks later, we had three players sent-off in a friendly game against London Welsh at Old Deer Park. It was the most violent friendly I have ever been involved in, and I've been involved in a few violent, friendlies in my time. Gareth and Glyn Llewellyn were both playing their first games for London Welsh and by the end of the game, I think they both wished they hadn't bothered.

Even though I was Captain and had led Newport through a very successful period in their history, I still didn't feel accepted by many of the committee. Because I didn't conform, they didn't really know how to handle me. For example, there was an unwritten rule that if you captained Newport Rugby Club you automatically got to play at Newport Golf Club.

Did they invite me? No.

Did I want to go play there? Did I hell, but that's not the point!

I loved a round of golf. Once, I was playing on a Sunday afternoon down in Peterstone. My ball went in near the edge of the water. As I was looking for it, I spied a trout swimming about in the lake. It was a beauty, about 4 lbs. I waded in to get my ball, and the trout kept circling around me. I had a quick look about to make sure no one was looking. I got my iron out and clubbed it with my first swing. If only I could have played golf as consistently. I grabbed the fish, wrapped it up in a towel and hid it in my golf bag. I didn't tell anyone. Later in the club, I got the chef to cook it up for me.

I don't know what it is with me and animals on golf courses. Another time, while playing at Sun City, South Africa, I again hit a wayward shot and my ball went down towards a lake. As I walked down to retrieve it, I could see a pair of eyes sticking out of the water. This time it wasn't a fish but a reptile in the shape of a bloody huge crocodile. It glared up at me. So, looking about to make sure no one could see, I stunned it and wrapped it in a large beach towel and hid it in my golf bag. I wish I had! But I did hit him on the head with a seven iron when it came running at me. I left my ball and ran like hell.

Thinking about it, maybe that's why the Newport committee never invited me to their golf club when I played for Charlie Faulkner RFC.

# 7

# The Cat With the Ten and A Half Inch Tail

*"It was a pleasure to welcome a player of Mike's stature to Newport RFC in 1982. He was an extremely committed and dedicated player who refused to be second best. He very quickly added steel, experience and leadership to our side. In 1983/84 Mike was elected Newport RFC 1st XV Captain and very quickly made a significant impact with his impressive leadership and motivational style, leading from the front. It was an honour to play with and be captained by Mike. He was an inspirational and supportive captain, and is still a very good friend. I admired and respected him so much that my wife and I agreed to name our son after him."*

**Roger Powell**
**Newport**

I had some memorable excursions around the world with Charlie and his Gwent rugby factory. Like Vikings, we ventured to faraway shores looking to conquer and pillage, and everything else in between. I had many bizarre and wonderful experiences, with Charlie never far from the action.

One of the craziest incidents happened in Portugal. On the rugby playing side, which is the worst part of any rugby tour, we faced their national team in Lisbon but on the social side, clearly the main reason for going there, we ate, drunk and partied in Estrada do Porto de Mos.

One morning after a heavy session, Charlie and I lay by the swimming pool in our hotel, Hotel Woodpecker. I'll never forget it. It wasn't the plushest place I'd ever been, a One Star joint at best. Similar to a doss house in Ebbw Vale, but with sunshine.

'Charl,' I said, 'I'm sure the water in the pool is lower than it was yesterday.'

He tutted.

'Spike, don't you know nothing. What's that up there?' he said sarcastically.

'Where?'

'Up there.'

'The sky.'

'No....not the sky...that?'

'A cloud.'

'No, there's no clouds up there. That?'

'The sun.'

He nodded. 'That's the reason. The sun is sucking all the water out of the pool. It then makes all the clouds and rain and stuff. That's what's happening.'

'But there's no clouds up there.'

He huffed and read his paper. With my geography lesson over, I went to the bar to get some drinks and told the boys about Charlie's revelation. Much later that same night, some of the team, me not included this time, honest, sneaked down to the pool and let all the water out.

It must have seemed quite a funny thing to do at three in the morning while tanked-up. However, in the warm light of a Portuguese morning, with small kids standing around with rubber rings on, crying, and angry parents looking for answers, it didn't seem so comical.

The hotel manager couldn't prove it was us. But he had his suspicions. He warned our committee that if anything else disappeared or got broken there would be trouble.

Charlie called me over, 'We have got to have some discipline with our boys, Spike.

'What do you suggest?'

'Let's get them all together later on and get them to march, army style, into the town. Get some discipline back in them.'

Dying to laugh, I rounded all the boys up in the pool room.

'Right,' Charlie said, 'we are all going to meet up later and we are all going to march into town together. We will all meet at,' He looked at his watch, 'fourteen hundred hours. For all you dull bastards that can't tell the time, that's four o clock!!'

We all fell about laughing.

True to his word, Charlie marched us all into town. 'Up, two, three, four, Up, two, three, four,' he did his Sergeant Major bit at the front, yelling at us all. We looked like a bunch of idiots, but we had a great *craic*.

Later that night, in the town, the team got split-up and I ended up walking the streets looking for something to eat with Phil Parks and Richie Collins, a policeman who had not long joined the club.

What we had failed to notice was the gang of local youths eyeing us up for most of the night. It turned out that many of the local trouble-makers were waiting for a chance to have a go at us. As the three of us walked down the street, about twenty of them came charging at us. We legged-it and jumped into a waiting taxi.

The mob surrounded the car.

'Go! Go! Go!' I yelled at the driver.

He sat there, scared stiff.

The back window got smashed-in as they pelted the car with sticks. Richie's arm was cut really badly. The taxi driver opened his door and disappeared sharpish. Fighting off a few of them, I clambered over into the driver's seat, started the engine and put my foot down. At that moment the windscreen imploded as a brick smashed through the glass. Without caring if I hurt anyone, I drove through the thugs, bowling them over like skittles. They chased us to the end of the street, but I drove away.

Somehow, I managed to get us back to the safety of the hotel. We sat in silence in the beaten-up car, realizing we had escaped a right good pasting and with Richie's arm bleeding quite badly.

'What are we going to do with the taxi?' I said, 'We don't want anyone to know it was us.' We were going home the following day, so I didn't want the hassle of police interviews and all that jazz. Knowing me, I would probably end up headline news in the local paper and get banned from somewhere or other!

'We will have to hide it,' Phil replied.

'Where?'

'In Charlie's room.'

The image flashed crossed my mind of Charlie and the taxi in bed together. The giant prop drinking tea in his pyjamas while trying to explain to the car how the sun gobbled up the water.

Jokes aside we still had the evidence to get rid of. Leading from the back of our hotel, down to the sea, was a boat ramp. I suggested we rolled it down and into the water, out of harm's way.

'They wouldn't find it, we'll be gone soon, so there will be no problem,' I reassured the others.

Why we just didn't push the taxi down the ramp, I really don't know. Maybe that would have been too easy. For some reason, I got back in and drove into the cold water, which quickly rose up inside the car.

Panic stations! I was stuck and couldn't get out. I tried to open the door but it wouldn't budge. The car sank deeper and deeper into the sea. I thought I was heading for an icy grave. Now that would have made an interesting front page for the Western Mail. In the end I swam out of the hole where the windscreen had once been.

Soaking wet, we searched the hotel for our first-aid man to sort out Richie's arm, but just when we thought we had got away with it, the police arrived in all their glory. They had put two and two together and decided it must have something to do with the foreign nutcases on top of the hill. The taxi driver pointed us out and the three of us were arrested. They locked us up in a smelly old cell. From the next cell some local thugs shouted threats and abuse through the metal bars.

Ritchie was worried that he could be in trouble if the news of our arrest got back to his police force.

'Nothing we could do,' I said, 'and anyway, we were attacked.'

The Newport committee arrived *en masse*, like the angels of doom. Brian Jones, the chairman, stood in front of us, shaking his head. 'What have you done this time Spikey?'

'Before you start, I haven't done naff all.'

'No,' he replied, 'you never do, do you?'

Outside our hotel he had watched in horror as the taxi was dredged from the sea with its windows smashed. There was blood all over the ramp and it led into the hotel. Brian later told me he thought I had murdered someone. What a great reputation I had!

After some good bargaining, we got off all charges but had to pay £1,000 damages for the inside of the taxi. The thugs who attacked us paid for the damage to the outside of the vehicle. Richie Collins swore he would never go on tour again with me!!

From the first time I met him, Charlie has always been fascinated by my cock. Not in a gay way. I don't think Charlie knew what gay actually meant. When he used to see it in the showers after games, he just shook his head before muttering, 'Good God, Spikey...It's a beaut, mun.'

It's not bad if I do say so myself.

Problem was, that particular part of my anatomy got me into more trouble than I care to remember. Although most of it was very, very enjoyable!

On a tour to Bermuda, during a drunken session in one of the local bars, Charlie thought he would show me off a little, and hopefully make a bit of money in the bargain.

He looked about the room. In the corner, a big ginger tom cat, with a big bushy tail, lay fast asleep.

'Tell you what, I bet you Spikey's old boy is bigger than your cat's tail.'

Everything in the bar stopped. Everyone glanced at the cat and then at me, and then down at my crotch. I could see people's eyebrow's rising up.

A smile crossed the barman's face, 'Ok, man, 50 dollars.'

'Bloody hell Charl,' I said. 'Are you serious.'

'Shut up Spikey.'

Too late to turn tail and get out of there. The bet had been made and money was laid out on the counter. I couldn't believe that here I was on tour, representing one of the biggest rugby clubs in the world and I had somehow got myself into a 'who's got the biggest cock/tail' competition with an unsuspecting tom cat.

'How are we going to measure them?' someone piped up.

As they all looked about for a stick or a plank of wood or something, the barman appeared holding a roll-up tape measure. The kind of tape a shop assistant in a tailors would have draped around their neck. With that problem solved, the next challenge was actually catching and measuring the cat's tail.

# THE CAT WITH THE TEN AND A HALF INCH TAIL

Like a pride of lions circling around their prey on the African plains, a few of the boys sneaked up on the sleeping feline, but the cat knew something was up. Using it's sixth sense, the creature opened one eye and leapt up just as a pair of hands went to grab it. They eventually caught it and pinned it down on the pool table. The cat fought like a wild banshee, its claws flailing about. It hissed and made the weirdest of noises.

'Ten and a half inches,' one of the boys announced before letting it go. It then went for one of them before darting out of the pub. Once again, all eyes in the bar glanced over at me.

I sat on the edge of the pool table, getting ready to get my weapon quantified.

After much stretching and pulling on my part, and to the obvious disappointment of Charlie, I came up just short. The barman grinned and reached over to retrieve his winnings.

'Hang on,' Charlie piped-up with a serious look on his big Bagpuss-face. 'We measured that cat from the tip of his tail to his arsehole...didn't we?'

The boy, with the tape, nodded, 'Yes, we did.'

'Yes, thought so.' Charlie turned to me. 'Spikey, get your trousers off and get back up on the pool table.'

'What?'

'You heard me.'

So there I was, a minute later, spread-eagled on the pool table, bollocks naked, legs up in the air, like the dying fly. Meanwhile, someone precariously placed the tape from the middle of my chocolate starfish to the end of my old boy.

A huge cheer went up as the result got announced. In the bright red corner, measuring in at a whopping.......I'm too shy to tell you. But let's just say, Charlie sat at the bar, smiling, 50 dollars better off that night.

I had my own back on Charlie a few months later, when we were down in Carmarthen doing a presentation dinner together. He was lying on his single bed, pissed-up, about 3am and still wearing his British Lion's blazer. I unzipped his trousers and carefully got his knob out. I then took the laces out of his shoes and tied them tightly together. After tying one end of the laces to his knob and the other to his wrist, I opened the door for a quick getaway, before whacking him on the head with a tray. I could hear his screams from way down the corridor.

Near the end of my career, my trouser snake once again almost got me into deep trouble. Although I wasn't on tour with Newport I was still playing for them. At the grand old age of 34, I captained a star-studded World Sevens Team playing in Durban, South Africa. The team included the likes of David Campese and some of the best sevens players in the world.

After the match, a big dinner had been arranged with over 400 guests including the President of the SARFU and his wife. Also there was the beautiful Miss Jarpie, who was Miss South Africa at that time. As usual, after the game I took hold of the after-dinner entertainment by the scuff of the neck. For a laugh I decided to hold a raffle. What no one knew was I had cut a hole in the raffle box. I put my old boy in it and covered it with the raffle tickets. A childish prank I know, but a funny, childish prank all the same. My aim was to call Miss World up on stage and have her rummage about in the box. Unfortunately, she wouldn't come up.

There I was on stage in front of a room filled with important people with my old boy resting neatly inside the box. To my horror, the wife of the President of the SAFR walked onto the stage and put her hand in. She touched my pride and joy and screamed, 'There's a mouse. There's a mouse in the box.'

Jokingly I whispered, 'Say it's a rat for God's sake...say it's a rat.'

She gave me a real stinking look. I thought, 'Shit I could

be in trouble here'. Waving my tool about in Crumlin rugby club had often been considered a *craic*. However, out in South Africa, maybe they wouldn't appreciate someone hiding their todger in a box so it could get groped by the wife of a VIP. What I considered to be a laugh looked like it could get me a tiny cell on Robben Island opposite Nelson Mandela for a thirty year stretch. Now and then I did things without considering the outcome. I shiver now when I think back to the things I got away with.

Back on the stage, still holding the box tight against my lower regions, I shuffled off. I rushed behind a curtain and made myself decent again, before walking back in as if nothing had happened.

For my last tour with Newport, I wanted us to go somewhere trendy with lots of drink and hot women and not particularly in that order. Ayia Napa in Cyprus sounded like the perfect destination. I'd made my mind up I was leaving the club, so I didn't want to play on tour. I'd had a gut's full by then. I just wanted to relax and have a laugh.

Walking around the town, Charlie insisted he wanted to buy his wife a dress.

'No Charl, buy her something else,' I pleaded, 'the worst thing you can do is buy clothes for a woman. She's not going to like whatever you get. Women are different to men. Different tastes to us.'

'Oh no Spike,' he drawled, 'Gill always likes me picking her clothes.' I took one look at what he was wearing and said, 'I bet she does, but no Charl. Honestly, pick something else.'

With his mind already made up, he stared at a dress in a shop window. 'Do you think she will like that?'

I shook my head. 'It's a bit old fashioned Charl.'

He growled at me. 'Spikey, what does it say above the shop window?'

'It says boutique,' I replied.

'See,' He said. 'It's a Bo-Teek. If it's a Bo-Teek, it can't be old fashioned. It's got to be modern.'

I had to sit down on a bench because I was laughing so much. 'Ok Charl but what size is she?'

'I don't know.'

'How are you going to buy her a dress if you don't know her size?'

Again, I could see the cogs in his mind ticking over. He looked about. 'Well, she's about the same size as Jamesy.'

We all turned and looked at the No 10.

'Try the dress on Jamesy,' I demanded.

'Are you serious?'

I nodded.

'I'm not doing it.'

'Just get it on Jamsey, and no complaining.'

After some persuading, the outside half came out wearing the dress.

'I'm not sure Charl, maybe if he had high heels on I could tell,' I joked.

To the great delight of the shop owners, Jamsey ended up parading around the shop dressed up like a woman without a wig. Charlie bought it.

I saw Gill a few weeks after we came back. 'Why the hell did you let him do it, Spike? Why?'

I just shrugged.

After our shopping trip we headed back to the apartments to see what the rest of the boys were getting up to. Eddie Brookes from Ebbw Vale was one of those guys who would try anything once, and if he liked it, knowing Eddie, more than once. He lives in El Salvador now, enough said.

In his room, a gang of boys lay about, laughing their heads off.

'Why are they all laughing, Spike?' Charlie asked.

His words made them laugh even more. I soon guessed they must have taken something they shouldn't have.

'Magic mushrooms,' one of them whispered to me.

Apparently, Eddie had been cooking up omelettes and sprinkling the hallucinating mushrooms on top. Drugs have never been my thing, and never will. I haven't got anything against people who do drugs, it's up to them. They can do what they want. They're just something that have never interested me.

I knew Charlie hated drugs as well. But he didn't know what the hell was going on.

'Fancy a nice fresh omelette, boys?' Said Eddie cracking some eggs into a frying pan.

I winked at Eddie.

'Oh, I love an omelette me,' piped up Charlie.

'No way Charl, you can't have one,' I insisted.

'Come on Spikey...let me have one.'

'No Charl...we've just had breakfast.'

'That was ages ago,' Charlie licked his lips.

Then Eddie chipped in. 'Oh go on let him have one.'

In the end I played along, 'Ok make him one. What do you want on it, Charl, extra mushrooms?'

Charlie's face lit up. 'Oh yea, I love mushrooms, pile them on, Ed. Pile them on.'

The boys couldn't breathe from laughing so much. The egg feast didn't touch the sides. Charlie wolfed it down in about three bites. Then we all waited for the show to begin. We sat there watching him, trying not to give the game away.

'That was lovely. The best omelette I've ever had.'

Twenty minutes later, he began laughing like the Penguin from the Batman films. He didn't stop for about two hours. He tried to be serious but he couldn't.

'What you laughing at, Charl?'

'I don't know, Spike.' He laughed louder.

Then he had a bit of a low point and got so paranoid that he locked himself away in his room and refused to answer the door. He emerged hours later.

'Fancy a mushroom omelette Char,' I joked.

'Where's bloody Eddie?' Charlie stormed out.

# 8

# The Irish Generation Game

*"I remember his first game as captain against Ireland in Lansdowne Road, very well! It was a difficult place to win but we managed to do so thanks to Spikey's leadership. That day we would have followed him 'into battle' anywhere.*

*Spikey was a great leader who every passionate rugby player would follow; a fine leader of men who retired from international rugby far too early!"*

**Rob Ackerman**
**Newport - London Welsh - Wales - British Lions**

Although my performances for Newport got me a number of good reviews, as far as another call up into the Welsh squad was concerned, I was still very much out in the cold. In fact, after my enforced, four-year sabbatical, it felt as if I was sat in an igloo at the North Pole, in my underpants, with my feet in a bucket of ice cubes.

Repeatedly I was told by eminent individuals at the WRU that no matter how well I played, I would never again wear the red shirt. That was so hard to take when I knew that other players who had been involved in incidents on and off the field had been accepted back.

Mentally, it almost broke me. I went through more ups and downs than most. Family and friends helped me through the pain. I don't know how they put up with me on times. They kept me going and kept me focused when the rest of Wales ignored me.

Like I said, Charlie always had great faith in me. I think he saw me as his prodigal son. He banged on the door of the WRU constantly, pushing my case as far down their throats as he could get away with.

'You're playing well Spike, they'll have to pick you.' He encouraged and supported me every step of the way. My very own personal 18 stone door-to-door canvasser. He managed me pretty well. As well as anyone could, I guess. After each game he would say, 'Now don't do anything daft now, Spike. Just have a few drinks and then go home.'

If he had had his way, as soon as the whistle went, he would have put me in a straitjacket and locked me in a padded cell until the next game. Perhaps that's what I needed.

Yet deep down I knew I wasn't that bad a person, in any way, shape or form. I liked a laugh, and a bit of fun. I admit I had an edge to me at times, which could be 'spikey' to say the least. But that was me, Spikey by name and 'spikey' by nature.

The people pulling the selection strings didn't want to forgive and forget though. It got to the point where I firmly believed if I was the last hooker left standing in Wales, and all the others had been mysteriously killed in some tragic hooker-related plane accident, they still wouldn't have selected me.

Then came a stroke of luck. Steve Jones, the Pontypool hooker, was sent off in a club game, and I heard on the grapevine that I had been picked to sub against Japan for an uncapped game. I switched on the news to see if all the other hookers in Wales had actually been killed in some tragic hooker-related plane accident. They hadn't been!

'Bloody hell' I thought. Although keeping the bench warm yet again wasn't what I had in mind, I didn't complain. At least, my foot, or just say my big toe, was poking back in through the door.

After watching the match from the Arms Park bench I didn't know if I wanted to be back or not. Wales were terrible. No direction, no style, no fight or fire in their bellies. We just managed a two point victory.

It didn't end there. Next I got invited to train with the team in preparation for a game against Romania at the end of November 1983. I knew that as soon as I got to a training session I would get in the Welsh side. I just knew it.

Charlie Faulkner raced around to my house as soon as he heard the news. 'Spikey, do me a favour now will you,' he said in his deep, Newport drawl.

'What is it, Charl?'

'When you go training, keep your gob shut when you get there, and you'll be ok.'

'Of course I will. I'm not an idiot.' I said.

I'm not sure who smiled the widest!

It felt so good to be warming up on the Arms Park once more. It had been a long five years out in the wilderness and I didn't think I would ever be allowed to put my feet on the hallowed turf again. All the big names were there jogging about. Robert Norster, David Pickering and the others.

As we trained, I couldn't help noticing how everybody just seemed to be moaning and groaning. It was all 'What are we doing here.' 'It's bloody cold.' 'We're only playing Romania.'

I kept my head down, gob shut and did the session. Charlie would have been proud. It went well. I've always been quite proud of my fitness, so that part of it wasn't an issue. Although I was touching thirty, I was still extremely fit.

After the session, just under the stands, Clive Rowlands led a discussion about what went wrong the week before.

'Has anyone got anything to say?' he asked.

I stood there biting my lip. I thought I'd better not say anything; I didn't want to upset the apple cart. Some of the stars were still moaning about this and that and blaming everything under the sun for the poor performance.

I put my hand up. I couldn't help it. The little devil inside me popped out and sat on my shoulder. He wasn't the only one pissed off.

'What is it Spikey?' Clive asked.

'Look. I've been waiting five years to get my chance again. Five years dreaming for this opportunity, while they are moaning about that.' I could feel their eyes burning into me. Under their breath they must have been hissing, 'Oh here he goes, Spikey's off on one again.'

I went for it, tongue blazing. 'There are people who would give their right and left arm to play for Wales and you guys haven't stopped bloody complaining. You should take a long, hard look at yourselves.' I shook my head and headed down the tunnel.

I didn't go straight home. I went to Charlie's.

'How did it go, Spike?' He asked as he handed me a chocolate Hobnob.

'Fitness went well, no problem.'

'Great. Great. I knew you could handle it,' he said. 'You didn't do anything stupid did you? You didn't say anything out of order, did you?'

Sheepishly I turned, 'Well I did actually Charles.' I then told him what I'd said and why I'd said it. 'What would you have done?'

'I would have done the bloody same, Spikey. They're a big bunch of moaning bastards.'

Even with my outburst, I still got to travel out for the Romania game. I didn't realise how bleak Romania was until we landed there. Everything seemed to be in black and white. I saw more horses and carts than I did cars. Our hotel was decent enough, although the food took some getting used to. It was before the days when teams took their own cooks with suitcases full of pasta and Jaffa Cakes. Everyone had the trots within twenty four hours of touching down.

My funniest memory of the entire trip was an incident that saw Barry John getting fleeced of his money. I love Barry to bits. Even in my darkness days, he was one of my true supporters and always shouted my praises from the rafters.

On the trip, the great outside half came along wearing his reporter's hat. Before leaving Wales, we had been warned not to change money because the rate was so bad there. Their money was more or less worthless. Instead, someone told us to take items like women's tights or cigarettes and bars of chocolate to trade for different things. I didn't fully believe it, but I filled my suitcase up with goodies just in case. I packed away a couple of Cadbury cream eggs and a few Crunchies. I thought, if they don't get me at least a blow job, nothing would.

It appeared that Barry John didn't know about the money situation. One afternoon, while walking down the street, he heard a loud, 'Pssh...oh mister do you want to change some money.' He told us later, a stereotypical Eastern European bloke materialised from a doorway, wearing a big leather coat and sporting one long bushy eyebrow. King Barry followed the right shifty geezer down an alley-way, where he handed over about five hundred pounds in return for a huge wadge of Romanian money in a shoe box with an elastic band around it. Honest to God.

Barry came back to the hotel to count it. I could see his face change. What 'One Eye Brow' had done was use real money for the top half inch and the bottom of the stack of cash. The majority of the 'money' in the middle was just paper, like something you'd see in a 'heist' movie. Barry had fallen for it, hook, line and sinker. It cheered me up for a while.

The night before the game, bored and restless, I'd heard a rumour one of the players was entertaining a lady of the night in his room. For a laugh, I blagged a spare key from reception and sneaked into the pitch-black room, where I could hear the bed springs creaking. All of a sudden, a bright, red glow lit up the woman's face. Then it went dark again. It happened a few more times. What the hell was going on? I switched on the light. The player, who will remain nameless was on the bed with the hooker, who looked at least 80! Positioned on all fours, she crouched like a jackal, smoking a cigarette and looking thoroughly bored. I half expected her to be peeling spuds as well for the family dinner. She didn't blink an eyelash and just carried on smoking.

The game itself in Bucharest proved to be even more pitiful than the shambles against Japan and we lost 24-6. I must say, a little part of me was kind of pleased. I know that's a dreadful thing to say about your country, but I knew there would be one hell of an outcry back home, with the public wanting heads to roll.

Something needed to be done. Not only did we lose but the guys out on the field got beaten up in all departments. The Romanians proved to be a tough old outfit, but we showed no heart, no commitment, no anything. Simply put, there had been lots of bad selections and no one seemed to be playing for the shirt.

It proved a shattering experience for all concerned, especially the Captain, Eddie Butler. After the game he wandered around the hotel whiter than a ghost. Big, grey clouds descended over the entire squad. Everyone wore long faces and sat in small groups in silence. No one dared smile or crack a joke.

'Come on,' I told Eddie, 'It's not the end of the world. We'll get stronger after this.'

I took it upon myself, to do whatever I could to lift the spirit of the team. I gathered all the players together and locked them away in one of the function rooms in the hotel. They sat there as if in a mortuary. My task was to bring the players back to life. I ordered a shed-load of beers, launched into a bit of a stand-up routine and got everyone involved. I even made the six new caps do a solo spot each. It worked to a degree. I wouldn't say it made everyone strip off and swing from the chandeliers, but it lightened the mood a little.

I must have been on top form because, for the first time ever, one or two of the committee thought I was more than just a trouble maker.

Then the test came.

A few hours later, by the bar, some pissed-up, cocky Romanian, dressed like a hobo, plonked himself right in front of me. He stood there, blowing cheap-smelling cigarette smoke into my face. Everyone stopped and stared. Some players put their hands over their faces. They knew what was coming. However, they didn't expect a new Spikey to emerge. I smiled at the bloke and walked away. I knew if I had punched him, and I really wanted to, it would have meant *sine die* for me. Banned forever. The cynical part of me wouldn't be surprised if some Welsh Rugby Union official hired the idiot to pick a fight with me. To push me to the limit to see if would lose control, and do something daft. This time, however, I didn't take the bait. Instead I went looking for the 80 year old chain-smoking, potato-peeling whore, only joking!

Back in Wales, the press and fans took no prisoners with their criticism. They tore the side, and especially Eddie, to pieces and things got way too personal. Many of the fans thought Eddie shouldn't even have been in the side, never mind the being the captain.

It was a difficult time for Welsh rugby. The loss highlighted the fact there was little direction and too much in-fighting throughout the sport. Not for the first time, we were the laughing stock of the world game. Something needed to be done to save the Whales, no sorry, Wales.

I hoped I would be part of the revolution, but feared I probably wouldn't be.

Then, one of the biggest surprises of my rugby life occurred. I was asked to captain the B team out in France. Believe it or not, the B team were worse than the National side. They had lost five of their previous six games without scoring a try. On top of that, they hadn't won in France in the last seven attempts, and again hadn't scored a single try.

So, not much pressure on the captain then!!

Although it appeared an impossible role, it was just the challenge I looked forward to, to prove my doubters wrong. I knew I needed to inspire the boys. The team had lacked leadership against Japan and Romania. Hopefully, I could bring that inspiration. I was now a calmer and wiser person. Well, that's what I told the press. Being captain of Newport had brought more control and responsibility to my game, on and off the field.

With the Five Nations Championship starting in a few months, I thought one good performance could bring me the unthinkable, to play for Wales. I began to plan what I wanted. In my mind, my biggest hurdle would be convincing everyone in our changing room we could not only win the game, but win it well. Many Welsh sides have gone to France and lost even before they actually got off the aeroplane. They lacked belief, but I didn't. I had buckets full of it.

I wanted us to lay down a marker, and restore some pride back in Wales. We were down in the gutter. We couldn't get any lower, unless we lost to Penarth! I wanted to bring us some respectability again and I really didn't care how we did it. Win, lose or draw, we were going to be a totally committed side on the field. Even if it meant every one of us getting sent off, carried off on stretchers or carted off by the French police.

I told my team when, not if, we won, the sky would be their limit. There would be opportunities in the senior squad up for grabs for them all.

On the Friday we stayed in Bourg-en-Bresse, a quiet provincial town overlooking the Alps close to the Swiss border. Not the best place for me to be holed up. I thought I would go off my head. Staring at my bedroom wall, I knew if I didn't get out of there I would end up doing something stupid like throwing a piano out of a bedroom window, or running around the hotel in the nude.

I rounded the players up. I told the committee, they were all bored and I was taking them to see the sights for a bit of team bonding. They didn't mind, they were all in the bar, getting the free drink down their necks. I took the players around the corner and straight into a café bar.

'Ok,' I shouted, 'lets have a couple of beers.'

'No, we can't,' someone replied.

'Oh, I'm Captain and I'm telling you now, we are ALL having a few beers and we are ALL going to let our hair down a little'

One or two beers weren't going to hurt us. We'd been training hard. The team looked in good condition. I ordered 10 pitchers of beer. It was kind of weird, watching grown men acting like underage teenagers having their first drink in some bar in their hometown.

Everyone seemed to enjoy it. I ordered another round of pitchers. We had a *craic*. Lots of laughing and larking about; and even a little sing song broke out. God knows what the French people in the bar thought. But no one got pissed, far from it. Just four or five glasses each but it did us all the power of good.

We all knew it was going to be a tough match. Full-on intimidation from the first whistle to the last. I wanted us to be a team. To be, and to feel, like a top-notch club side.

One player piped up, 'Spikey, do you think we'll beat them tomorrow?'

I stood on the table, 'I guarantee you we will beat them tomorrow.' I had no doubt. It was 15 players against 15. So why couldn't we beat them? I looked every one of my players in the eyes to make sure they were up for the fight. The door had been opened for me, for us all really, after being shut and bolted for years and no one was going to slam it shut on me again.

The next morning was freezing cold. A chilling wind whistled down from the nearby Alps. The ground was almost unplayable but I wouldn't have cared if we had been playing on top of Everest. As soon as I got out on that field all of my worries, and the drama of recent years, slipped off my shoulders. I wasn't one of those Captains who just liked to talk the talk; I made sure I walked it as well. I like to think I lead by example. The players responded, and more than stood up to the challenge.

At halftime we were losing, but had played alright. I got the players in a tight circle. 'Come on guys we can do this. We can be men and win this match.'

They didn't let me down. In the second half we completely dominated them. We smashed them up in their own backyard. We even scored a pushover try. The French team wilted like flowers. They had expected us to roll over and cry, but we were more than a match for them.

In the end, we won convincingly 23 to 11, scoring 4 tries. It would have been more of a massacre if we'd kicked all our conversions.

I must say, it felt good when the final whistle sounded. Whatever I've played in my life, I've always played to win. I don't subscribe to all this nonsense about 'losing will do a team good'. No, winning does a team good. Winning is everything. We were the first B side to have won out there and we won well. I believe we still hold that record to this day.

It felt nice to put some badly-needed pride back into Welsh rugby. Our biggest critic was the Welsh nation itself, and rightly so. But I knew from playing week-in, week-out, that Welsh rugby wasn't in that bad a state.

My emotional post-match team talk thanked all my players for their great effort and what they had achieved for Wales. 'The selectors will have to pick you now. You've set down a marker, staked a claim and got a great result!' I proudly stated.

One player questioned me directly, 'will they pick you now, Spike?'

'No chance. They won't pick me,' I replied, 'if I was the last hooker left standing.'

After the game I received a telegram of congratulation from my team mates at Newport and one from the Cardiff club.

The headlines in the Western Mail the next day stated, *'Watkin's heroes restore Welsh pride. Kids shows old guard the way.'* It continued *'It was a team victory of tremendous spirit that ran right through the side. Watkins, the outstanding hooker and forward in Wales, barked out commands and encouragement like a man possessed.'*

Overnight, I went from number one villain to superhero in the eyes of the press. Beating France over there had strengthened my cause and a groundswell of popular support now demanded that I play for the National side. I became the People's Choice, 'a ray of light to help brighten up our darkness,' someone said on the radio. Even some of the great golden oldies like 'Merv the Swerve' banged the drum for me as hard as they could.

I can only begin to imagine how the Welsh selectors felt. I bet they had many a sleepless night. By picking me for the French game they had unwittingly brought a monster back from the dead to haunt them.

For once I kept quiet. I sat back and watched from afar. I was now older and more philosophical about everything going on around me. But make no mistake, I still had ambition and I never gave up fighting for that red jersey. To do it though, I needed to leapfrog some good hookers like Steve Jones of Pontypool, Billy James of Aberavon, Mike Richards of Neath and of course, Mister Goody Two Shoes, Alan Phillips.

With a wave of support building for me, the WRU swayed a little, but not too far. They picked me for the senior team, but again only to warm the bench, for the first Five Nations match against the Scots in Cardiff.

After another lacklustre performance, we got well beaten. The coaches, John Bevan and Terry Cobner, told the press, that drastic change was needed. What else could they say? With pressure mounting, they knew one more loss would see them axed.

Rumours circulated they were about to drop the whole front row. Hooker Billy James was a decent enough guy but, in my opinion, just wasn't good enough to play at that level.

Not only were the national papers screaming for me to play, many were also looking for me to take over the Captaincy from Eddie. For once the smile on my face was as wide as the Taff.

To be honest, it felt good. I knew I was close, within touching distance. But I still didn't think it would come. My mind played tricks. Knowing my luck, I imagined them wheeling Bobby Windsor out from his retirement home before picking me. Or they would hire some rugby-crazed, mad scientist to make a super human hooker out of spare body parts. Dr Franken-hooker to the rescue!

The following Monday I was down in West Wales, delivering steel to Swansea docks when I got a message to call my wife immediately. I thought something was wrong with the kids, maybe an accident or something.

My wife's voice shook as she read the letter which said I had been selected to play against Ireland. Later that night I was called by the chairman of selectors. He told me that they acknowledged my leadership qualities as much as my playing ability.

'That's great,' I said, 'so am I captain?'

From the silence on the other end, I guessed he was completely taken aback. After a pause he said, 'No, Eddie is still captain.

'If I'm not captain, I don't want it.' I said, thinking 'what the hell, if they want me, I'm doing it on my terms.'

He paused again, then said he would come back to me. He hung up.

Ten minutes later, he called me back to congratulate me on the captaincy. I couldn't believe I had finally done it. I replaced Billy as hooker and Eddie as captain in my first international.

My selection must have caused lots of heated debates behind closed doors. Terry Cobner, the coach, was Pontypool through and through. He played for them and still had links to the club, where Eddie was club captain. He and Eddie used to travel together in the car for training in Cardiff. John Bevan, the other coach, was from Aberavon, Billy James's club.

I'm not sure even then if I was their first choice, or if they'd bowed to the pressure from the media and the man on the street. John Bevan never said a word to me when I was made Captain. Even in training, he never spoke. It wasn't an atmosphere I felt comfortable in, but I had been in worse situations. Terry Cobner warmed to me a little. They never asked me my thoughts. I didn't want to select the team, but it would have been nice to have sat down and had a chat about the previous game, and asked me what I thought.

On the other hand, I received support from people across Wales. Sacks full of cards arrived from all over the country, and beyond. I was going to be the first player to captain the side on his debut since the great Clive 'bring me a gin and tonic every fifteen minutes' Rowlands in 1963, when he captained Wales against England but lost. Apart from us, only three other players had achieved that feat. The others were:

- 1881 – James Bevan (Cambridge University) – played against England and lost.
- 1882 – Charles Lewis (Llandovery) – played against Ireland and won.
- 1934 – John Evans (Newport) – played against England and lost.

By becoming captain I took hold of the hottest potato in the world of rugby. In the previous few years, no one had really grabbed it and been dominant. Four captains had been used and discarded in three years, eight in all since Phil Bennett had hung up his boots in 1978.

I liked Eddie Butler, and still do, but in my opinion he wasn't the inspirational type of leader the team required, especially when things weren't going well. There was a lot of talent in the side, but none of the players seemed to be playing to their full potential.

Part of me would have liked to have played without the pressure of the captaincy. I could have just concentrated on doing my job. But deep down I wanted to lead the team out. I wanted to call the shots and lead from the front. In my mind, if I could handle a 36-ton juggernaut, I could tackle a job with one of the highest casualty rates in sport. I knew I could make a difference; put aggression back into the players and the smile back on the faces of the public.

I had never given up, even at my lowest point. I'd hit many lows points but I knew if I'd packed it all in, the WRU would have won. They would have beaten me, and I couldn't have that. I wanted to take them on.

What made me laugh, were the false crocodile smiles on their faces once the news was announced. They stood there patting me on the back, and wishing me luck. For five previous years, those WRU Committees had been sticking daggers deep into my flesh and taking great pleasure in twisting them. I would like to say it didn't bother me, but I'm human after all.

Now the wheel had turned full circle. A case of the poacher turned gamekeeper. A sweet taste when it came, although it had been coated in effort and heartache. Really, it should have been my 31$^{st}$ cap, not my first. After I got myself banned, Phillips went on to have 19 of my caps and Billy James the other 11.

I didn't let the pressure get to me. It was just another game. Because of my involvement in the Welsh squad in the 1970's I'd been there long before any of the current squad members. Although it was my first cap, I was probably the most experienced player in the side, the sole survivor from the Triple, Triple Crown days.

The Thursday before the game, I worked a 10-hour shift, came home and locked up my truck for the weekend. I drove down the Valleys in my silver Rover to Cardiff, *en route* to Dublin.

As soon as I arrived, I arranged a meeting with the players. I spoke from my heart. I never wrote things down. I have always been passionate, so words just flow. I wasn't a bang-the-walls type of Captain. If needed, I told certain individuals some home truths, but without getting too personal. I wouldn't think twice about calling them a gutless bunch of so-and-so's if I thought it would help our cause. It wasn't a problem to me.

The players accepted me straight away. They had played against me over the years. They knew what I was made of. I didn't care what they thought of me as a person. But they knew that, as a rugby player, I always gave 100% from the first whistle until the last. Other teams would have needed a Gatling gun to stop me trying to win and even then they'd have to make sure I was dead.

Ireland was going to be a true baptism of fire and the team needed everyone rowing in the same direction so I called Eddie Butler up to my room for a quick meeting. As I said, I liked Eddie. Even today, I see him around at different events, and we always have a chat. I think he had a rough ride with the Welsh public. They always saw him as this middle class twit, more English than Welsh. But to me he was a solid bloke. No one got to play for Pontypool during Prosser's reign if they didn't have something about them. Enough said.

'Look Eddie,' I was open and to the point, 'you've had your chance and you messed it up. Now I hope you ain't going to mess it up for me.'

To be fair to Eddie, he replied by saying, 'No, Spike I'm on your side, I will totally support you in whatever way I can', and that he did. Many said, and I think Eddie would admit it himself; he played much better when he didn't have the weight of Captaincy and the hopes of an entire country resting on his shoulders.

Obviously Charlie was chuffed to bits. He couldn't stop smiling all week. He came to see me before we left for Ireland.

'Do me a favour now, Spike, its very important.' He said, deadly serious. I thought he was going to say something really sensible like 'make sure you keep out of trouble' or 'go to church'. 'What favour?' I asked.

'Look Spike, whenever I played against Ireland and stayed in the Shelbourne Hotel in the city centre; after breakfast, I would take some bread and go feed the ducks in the park opposite in St Stephen's Green.' I waited for the punch line. 'Every time I did it, we won out there. So if you do that, we will win....mark my words.'

'You must be joking, Charl.' I said.

'Remember when you were sub? I did it then.'

He was right. The last time I'd been to Dublin and sat on the bench in 1976, we'd won. So to stop him nagging, I said I would carry out his black, duck magic but I had absolutely no intention of going through with it. I simply didn't believe in all that hocus pocus stuff. However, on that misty Saturday morning, while sitting down to have breakfast, I looked at the bread rolls in the basket and then out at the park opposite. Charlie's face and his words spun around in my head like the wizard from the Wizard of Oz. 'Feed the ducks...feed the ducks and we will win....win.....win.'

I knew that if we'd lost, the whole country would jump off the edge of a cliff into the Irish Sea. We were heading for our worst and blackest record in modern times. I'm not superstitious, but I must admit that I did pop quite a few bread rolls into my pockets and went for a walk to say hello to the ducks.

For me to lead the team out at Lansdowne Road was the stuff of fairy tales and legends. No one in the crowd of over fifty thousand gave us a hope in hell of keeping the scores close, never mind winning. To add to our woes, our only true world superstar, Terry Holmes got injured and wasn't available.

Despite the odds stacked against us, I was still quietly confident of causing an upset. I knew we had a massive mountain to climb, but I believed we had a set of players who weren't afraid to give it a go, and scale the bloody thing. Plus, I had fed Charlie's ducks, so a win was in the bag!

Against the Scots there had been a few punches thrown, hand-bags at ten paces kind of stuff. I warned my players that, not if, but when, it kicked off, they had better be ready for it. 'Knock their fucking heads off,' were the words I think I used.

Like most internationals, the game would be won if we could win the battle up front. I knew if we matched and beat them where it mattered, we would be alright. Our backs were quite tasty, and could hold their own against any in the Championship. We also had a plan not to give away stupid, kickable penalties. Ollie Campbell, the Irish outside half, had emerged as a deadly kicker and he would certainly punish us at every opportunity.

From the kick off, my boys breathed fire. Our performance brimmed full of pride and passion. All my years of pent up emotion and frustration, bubbled up inside of me. All the disappointments, the heartache, and all the Caps I should have won.

I wanted to lead by example and keep a cool head. Their Captain, and British Lion hooker, Ciaran Fitzgerald was a player I respected. But respect is given before and after but never during a game. British Lion or not, I was going to make sure it wasn't easy for him.

Nine minutes into the match, they collapsed the scrum on purpose. Rather than complaining I saw it as my opportunity. Without going into graphic detail, let's just say, Fitzgerald didn't get back up again for a long, long time. When he did, blood poured from a wound by his ear and eye. Not knowing where he was, he hobbled off, his head cocked to one side. I could sense the selectors in the crowd, saying, 'Oh no, that bloody Spikey's been up to his old tricks again.'

I didn't care. From that moment, each of my players grew a few inches taller in stature. I had laid down a marker. We weren't there to make up the numbers.

Did I have any regrets for him 'bumping his head on the ground?' Not one. He was on the wrong field at the wrong time. If Mother Theresa had been in front of me, she would have gone home in an ambulance as well. It was nothing personal, only a case of doing what was needed to secure the victory.

Charlie always told me to remember the eleventh commandment, 'Thou shalt not get caught', and I hadn't. In those days, it was par for the course. If your side of the scrum went down you were going to get a shoe-ing. It made us better scrummagers. No way would we ever have purposely collapsed a scrum on a wet, Wednesday night under the lights in Pontypool Park. I wouldn't have been able to comb my hair for a month. I watch rugby today, and often they have scrum after scrum collapsing. Eating up the time and making the game boring. I'll tell you now, if every time they did it, they got the Pontypool treatment, they wouldn't go down again. It would make for a much better, faster and more enjoyable game.

Other than watching Fitzgerald getting helped off, the best part of the game was when old 'coffee-table arse' Rob Ackerman sold the most outrageous dummy I've ever seen to slice their midfield in two and score under the posts. I always joked that his arse was so huge, he could hold a Thursday afternoon women's coffee morning around it. But what a try!

We took on all the elements, the Irish weather, their 'Garryowens' and their passionate fans, and ended up winning eighteen points to nine. The last ten minutes were the longest I've ever played. They went on for what felt like hours. When the ref's final whistle sounded, I sank to my knees. It had been a long time coming for everyone. It hadn't been flamboyant but we'd won, which is never an easy thing to do in Dublin's fair city.

When it was over I couldn't wait for the proper celebrations to begin. What with it being my first cap, and a winning performance, the only player since 1882 to captain Wales on his debut and win, and our being in Ireland's capital; it was going to be a good night.

Then it all went a bit 'Irish.'

As we triumphantly strolled down the tunnel, a line of policemen stopped us entering the changing rooms. While the game was being played, someone had sneaked through the ventilation duct into our changing room and stolen some items. Obviously my first reaction was anger. I wanted to find out what was missing but as it was during the Troubles in Ireland, the Gardai were worried in case someone had planted a bomb.

We had been assured security would be tight and our dressing room guarded at all times. So how could a cat burglar squeeze through the sky light? It made me think, were the guards asleep, or had they sneaked out to watch the game or were they part of the scam?

They made us all go back out onto the field, in our cold and dirty kit, to wait while they did a bomb check. Fans still in the stadium wondered what the hell was going on. We stood around talking between ourselves. Then I had a brainwave.

I called the boys into a circle. 'Listen boys that was a great win today, brilliant. Remember this; it has been a lucky day for us, both on and,' I left a pause, 'off the field.' They didn't know what I was going on about. I added, 'we can make a few bob out of this. I know I've personally lost a lot of money today, a lot of money plus other valuable stuff.'

'How do you know, Spike?' someone asked.

'I'm telling you now, I just feel it. I feel like I've been robbed.' I winked at them. Some of them smiled knowingly. Others still didn't have a clue what I was on about. They were the ones definitely not from the Valleys.

When we had the all-clear to go back in, the fun began.

'I've lost a gold chain and about £150,' said Ian 'Ike' Stephens, to the Gardai, trying not to laugh.

Dick Moriarty stood next in line. 'I've lost about £200 and a gold chain and a really expensive watch.'

I could see Ikey thinking, 'bloody hell I forgot about a watch'. A couple more players told the police what they had lost, or supposedly lost. Only David Prickering, no sorry, Pickering said he hadn't had anything pinched.

By the time it came to me, I felt like I was a contestant on the Generation Game. 'I lost £250, plus a chain, plus a watch, plus a kettle and a cuddly toy.' I added, 'plus I had all the kitty money.' Dick smiled at me as if I was his hero. We didn't have any kitty money. We were lucky to get a beer token off the WRU never mind a kitty.

But, 'Hey Ho!' It's funny what can suddenly come your way!

Ikey Stephens stood there fuming because he had gone first. He wanted another bite of the cherry. If he'd had a moustache and a pair of glasses, I'm sure he would have run to the other end of the line and pretended he was another player. He couldn't hold back though. He piped up, 'Hang on...what I said about that money. I forgot I also had about 100 punts of Irish money.'

I burst out laughing. Even the policeman laughed. He knew the *craic* by then. He didn't care. He just wrote it down.

The WRU reluctantly gave us some money for the night. The only time I made money out of them. Plus later, the

Irish officials handed over a wadge of cash to compensate for what we had lost in what became known as the Great Rugby Robbery. I don't know to this day if that refers to the guy who had pinched it off us, or how we'd robbed it off the Irish Rugby Union.

When I got interviewed on TV, I said, 'It was the first time a winning team has said we were robbed!'

That night the news reported our win and, of course, how the Welsh team had been fleeced of hundreds of pounds and many priceless, personal belongings. The reports made it sound as if they had taken the crown jewels. In truth, all the burglar got away with was a couple of quid, a few cheap gold chains and probably watches he could have bought for a punt or two in any Irish garage. Part of me felt a little sorry for the low-life who had robbed us. There he was walking around Dublin with a few pounds in his pockets, while all the other criminals in the city must have been out searching for him, thinking he had struck gold.

The night got even more farcical. As you have read, I had been waiting for a long, long, long time to win my first Welsh cap. Now I had finally earned it, on the biggest sporting day of my life, the WRU didn't have a cap to give me.

Someone had forgotten it! Surely out of the three hundred and fifty WRU committeemen on the trip, at least one of them should have been given the responsibility of ensuring they packed everything. They must have had a checklist. Kit, check. Caps, check. Beer token, check. Brain cells, Uhmmmmm.

Subsequently, unlike every other new player, I had no cap awarding ceremony after the game. Surely they could have been a bit creative and wrapped someone's underpants up in Christmas paper and handed it to me or gone to a sports shop and got me a baseball cap, or maybe one of those caps with beer bottles on the top and straws on the side.

Alas, no. I had to wait for it. A week later, they posted it to me in a jiffy bag. What's more, they sent it to the wrong address. After years of waiting, training, blood, sweat and tears, Mrs Harris from Number 5 presented me with my first Welsh cap on a Saturday morning on my front door step, while I stood there eating toast in my underpants. I really kid you not!!!

To play for Wales is every Welshman's dream. It was my dream and I fulfilled it, but I didn't half feel like I was in some kind of bloody circus.

# 9

# A Bunch of Amateurs

*"There was never a dull moment when Spikey was around, both on the field and off. I shared a room with him on many occasions. He was, and still is, one hell of a boy. The incident with the Koala bear sums him up perfectly!"*

**Steve Fenwick**
**Bridgend - Wales - British Lions**

Being a proud Welshman, it is hard to put into words how it felt to run out in the red jersey before a packed house at the Arms Park for the first time, well, at anytime actually, and to do it as the captain and lead the team out is what dreams are made of.

After the win against the Irish, expectations in Wales reached fever pitch. I rode the wave of excitement as much as the next man and I couldn't wait to line up against the French.

But first off I needed to sort a little matter out. I plonked my birth certificate on the desk of the WRU Secretary Ray Williams to prove I was 30 and not 32 as they stated in the programme. I didn't want people thinking I was older than I was.

As for the two 'complimentary' tickets I was reluctantly given by the WRU, I handed them with pride to my old man. He didn't rip them up this time. Instead he simply gave them back. 'I have more important things to do,' he scolded.

All my life, people have told me how much of a gentleman my father was. They didn't see how hard he could be as well. Hard as nails at times.

Trying not to lose my temper, I replied, 'Dad you have no idea what it is like to play for Wales, have you? No idea what it would be like to run out onto the Arms Park?' He'd never watched me play even one game of rugby, which I guess is very unusual. In Wales, rugby is a religion and 99.9% of fathers would give their right nut to watch their son play for their country, never mind be captain.

Not my father. He looked at me and shrugged, 'No. No, I have no idea what it is like to play for Wales, or run out on the Arms Park, or play rugby with my mates. But what I can tell you is; when I went to Burma in the war, most of my mates didn't come back. You have your game to play, but just remember, it is only a game.'

Put like that, yes it was only a game, but it was an important part of my life. I wasn't fighting in any war, well not against another country for sure. I wanted to share the moment with him and my mother.

'They are taking the piss out of you,' he added, 'they always have and they always will. You have got to make a decision. It's either work with the trucks or the rugby.'

I didn't hesitate. I shook his hand. 'Sorry to say this Dad... but it's rugby for me.' I walked out. We parted company and I never worked for him again. We barely spoke after that, not until many years later.

We finally did get back together and said our piece. During our chat I said, 'Dad, do you realize how much I love you?'

He looked at me and muttered, 'You are not one of those homos, are you?'

I just shook my head and smiled. That's why I loved him.

As he got older, I think he began to realize how difficult it must have been for me, being torn between work, rugby and my family and everything else in the melting pot of the South Wales Valleys.

The most maddening part of all and the thing which even today I find hard to understand is that he really did bloody well care. After he died at the age of 78, I was cleaning out the bureau in his bedroom. When I was growing up it had always been locked and we were never allowed to go near it. Like I said, he never watched me play and never spoke to me about rugby. One of the drawers was full of his medals from the war and work stuff. Then in another drawer, I came across a folder. My hands shook so much when I opened it up that I dropped its contents all over the floor. It was full of all my press cuttings, everything I had ever done in my career, the good, the bad and the ugly. I had to sit down in the chair. Tears rolled down my cheeks.

I looked up to the heavens and screamed, 'You stupid bastard, why didn't you talk to me.' For some strange reason he had cut all ties with that side of my life. I didn't know if it was just a generational thing, or if we just couldn't communicate with each other. I feel so emotional just writing this part of the book.

Deep down, I really believe it was his way of trying to look out for me. It reminded me of the song *A Boy Named Sue* by Johnny Cash. I wondered if he did it to make me grow stronger and not to see me getting hurt by the establishment. Perhaps the same reason why he made me fight the boy in the back lanes years previously.

Being a regimental Sergeant Major, he knew I wasn't going to beat or break the establishment. I think he feared the worst, and in a bizarre sort of way, he wanted to lighten the load by telling me not to take it too seriously. Work was his life, his obsession in a way, but behind all that I finally knew he had been as proud as hell!

On saying that, I really wished he had been there to watch me lead out the team at the Arms Park. My mother came in her Sunday best. If I thought playing in Dublin was the best day of my sporting life, I was so wrong. Walking out of the tunnel and getting engulfed by a wall of noise will live with me until the day I die. Standing there and singing the National Anthem, while watching the passion in the faces of the fans felt so unreal, yet such an amazing privilege.

Other than the score line it was the perfect day. We lost, 16 points to 21, but we could have and should have won. It wasn't a typical dirty game, by French standards. We stood up to them toe-to-toe and Howell Davies missed a bucketful of kicks. I'm not blaming him, mind. I lost my temper at one stage when we had a kickable penalty. I threw a punch at my opposite number and the penalty got reversed. I felt terrible.

Although we got beat we did ourselves proud. Even their captain, the great Jean-Pierre Rives, said France were lucky not to have lost on the day.

Bitterly disappointed, at least we had the chance to make amends against the old enemy away at Twickenham in our next outing. Wales versus England! Whether it was for the Championship, the Wooden Spoon or just a race around the pub car park, it made the hairs on the back of my hands stand on end. It was the big one and as the saying goes in Wales, 'As long as we beat the English, we don't care'

Due to a neck injury sustained against the French, it had been touch and go if I could play or not, but there was no way I was going to miss this game. Terry Holmes came back into the side for this, our last game of the Championship and we were room mates at the hotel. He'd told me a big secret. He told me he was going to switch to rugby league at the end of the season. It would be a massive blow for Welsh rugby.

The night before the game, we stayed in Hedsor House in Maidenhead. Again, my worse fear surfaced - being shut away from the madding crowds with nothing to do.

'Let's go out for a pint, Terry,' I said.

'No Spikey, we can't. Don't mess it up again.'

'Just one. I'm bored.' I didn't really want a drink. I just needed to meet some normal people, and talk about normal things. I felt as if I was imprisoned in Colditz. I needed to break free. I considered tunnelling my way out from the bar using some teaspoons, but I bet the WRU had armed guards with dogs and spotlights surrounding the place.

'Remember the last time we went out in London?' Terry recalled the night the both of us hit the bright lights during a works trip. We ended up in some posh nightclub and I'd ordered and paid for a bottle of champagne. While the waitress went to get it, Terry had accidentally sat on and broken a glass on the table and cut his arse to shreds. Even though Terry was bleeding to death, I wouldn't leave until we got our money back for the champagne. He ended up having fifteen stitches.

'Ok, but lets just find a local and have one or two,' I pleaded.

After a lot of debate, however, Terry and the others persuaded me to stay and managed to keep me locked up safely in the hotel. I felt like the girl from The Exorcist who is tied to the bed. After my head spun around a few times, my inner demons finally cooled down enough to go to sleep, but it was a struggle.

After breakfast, we headed-off to Twickenham but to add to my pre-match tension, the bus got a puncture on the motorway.

The driver, who looked too old to change the programme on a TV remote, never mind the huge tyre, called his company to send someone out to change it.

'It will only take about an hour,' he said.

'An hour! I'm not sitting around on a bus for a bloody hour' I yelled, 'I'll end up killing someone.' I stared at the driver and then at the coach. I wanted us to get to the ground early to soak in the atmosphere.

'Where's the spare tyre, mate?' I asked him.

Off came my blazer. I got the jack out and changed the wheel myself on the side of the road. I can't imagine too many of the highly paid players of today doing that. Huge cheers greeted me when I got back on, full of grease and dirt. I didn't mind at all. It felt like I'd had a good warm up. In those days, teams didn't go out on the field to go through warm-up routines. Life was a lot simpler. We just crowded into a circle, counted to ten, for those in the team that could, and then steamed out onto the field for the battle to commence.

Arriving at the ground, felt like driving into a completely different world. The West Car Park was full of top-of-the-range BMWs and Rollers. People stood around in Barbour jackets eating finger food from hampers. The smell of cooked meat and the sound of champagne corks popping filled the air. Many of the English fans gave us the thumbs down sign. I felt like a Christian on my way into the amphitheatre to get eaten by lions. Others politely called us, 'inbreds' or 'sheep shaggers'. I didn't mind that, most of us were!

What gave the fixture an even greater edge than usual was it was being played out amongst the backdrop of the year-long Miner's Strike. I had just come from a village and a country where entire families were relying on food parcels and hand-outs to survive. The obvious division between the haves and have-nots was shocking.

I bottled it all in but it would soon come spilling back out. When we had changed, I cleared everyone except the players out of the changing rooms and sat them all down. 'Did you see all those posh twats out there with their posh cars,' I said. They all stared at me. My face glowed bright red. 'Listen to me now,' I almost screamed, 'Tomorrow, those bastards will still have their Rolls Royces. Tomorrow, they will still have their BMWs. Tomorrow they will still have their money, but let's fuck their day up today.' That was my 'we will fight them on the beaches' speech.

I was Winston Spikey Churchill and I would have played them all by myself if needed. I knew a win would mean everything to those miners fighting a bloody and cold war back home. An unfair war planned by Thatcher and her cronies against working people; my people. It would have been great if we could have marched out on the field wearing miners' helmets and carrying Davy lamps.

We received the usual boos and sheep noises when running out. Terry kept whispering, 'Michael John, keep it together. We'll do them.'

At the first lineout, I could feel my blood boiling. I threw the ball in and then leapt on Peter Wheeler, the English hooker, before smacking him one. He went down and for good measure, and for the hundreds of years of pain and suffering against the Welsh nation; I kicked him in the balls.

He looked at me and said, 'What was that for?'

'The fucking miners,' I spat back.

It set the tone. The rest of the boys were just as fired up.

Our game plan had been simple. Move the ball to our wingers, Adrian Hadley and Mark Titley, and we knew we would win. Bob Norster again proved a colossus in the lineout. We won every lineout for the first 20 minutes or so. When England did win one, all their supporters applauded as if they had scored a try.

Terry Holmes, as usual, was immense behind the scrum, a king amongst men, along with outside half, Malcolm Dacey who found gaps in their defence and dropped goals for fun.

A BUNCH OF AMATEURS

The confidence oozed through the side and in the end we destroyed them. They didn't have a look in. If the English had fielded two sides at the same time that day, they still wouldn't have beaten us.

Straight after the whistle and still buzzing from the victory, I got interviewed on the pitch by Nigel Starmer-Smith. He asked me how important the win was for me and for the whole of Wales.

'First thing Nigel,' I said, 'I would like to dedicate the win to all the miners who are out on strike in Wales. They are going through a very difficult time financially and emotionally with their families.' I looked straight at the camera and ended with, 'To all the miners out there, if you've got some money, go and have a few beers and enjoy this day, and I hope everything works out. That's how important it is to us all, Nigel.'

Many years later, I was in Aberfan for the 25$^{th}$ anniversary of that terrible disaster with the late, great Ray Gravell. Some of the old colliers at the event told me how they still remembered what I had said on TV all those years before, and how it had played a small part in keeping them going.

That's how important it was at that time, much more than a mere game. A guy called Tom Bellion actually wrote a poem about the game which he sent to me.

MIKE WATKINS - CAPTAIN OF WALES

Thank you, Spike Watkins
For what you have done
You rolled back the mists
And revealed us the sun

At that Twickenham game
No sign of a cloud

## SPIKEY – *2 Hard to Handle*

You buried the rose
In a funeral shroud

The cry of 'Brass handles!'
The two lovely drop goals
To Hell with the English
who went down with all souls

The years in the desert
Awaiting the call
To win treasured cap
This driver's long haul

I saw men drunk
And crying with pride
Thank you, again
And the boys in the side

Lovely Welsh girls
with a smile on their lips
Small, laughing children
with fried fish and chips

A long happy day
Then weary and tired
Give thanks to this man
A nation inspired

Tired, into bed
All happy and warm
To dream lovely thoughts
A nation reborn

TOM BELLION - WELSH RUGBY

Playing for Charlie Faulkner RFC

Leading the charge against Bath at the Rec with a certain Gareth Chilcott looking on.

## NEWPORT SEVENS TEAM
WINNERS OF SNELLING SEVENS TOURNAMENT, AUGUST 1985

S. PILL    A. COOMBS    D. WATERS    G. GEORGE    P. DANIELS

P. STEELE    D. ACKERMAN (Hon. Secretary)    M. J. WATKINS (Captain)    B. J. JONES (Chairman)    R. POWELL

Absent—P. TURNER    C. JONATHAN

Newport RFC's Snelling 7s winning team. Everyone said we could only play ten-man rugby but that wasn't the case!

In Bermuda during the ex-international 'Classic World Cup' in the mid-nineties. Left to Right: Me; Steve O'Donahue; Scott Thomas (Stan's son) and Charlie. It was a great trip and Wales won the tournament!

**Hooker Mike Watkins (Cardiff) manages to get front of the line possession although held by his opposite number Jean-Pierre Decrae. Referee Burnett of Ireland keeps a close watch.**

Playing against the French in a B International at Pontypool Park in November 1976. We won 24-6.

# CARDIFF RUGBY FOOTBALL CLUB

Hon. Secretary:
A. J. PRIDAY

General Secretary:
K. H. GEORGE
A. Heffell

President: Cardiff Athletic Club
L. M. SPENCE, Esq., M.B.E.

CARDIFF ARMS PARK
CARDIFF, CFI IJA

5th December, 1983

Mr Mike Watkins,
c/o Newport R.F.C.
Rodney Parade,
NEWPORT.

Dear Spike,

On behalf of the Chairman and Committee of your
'Old Club' may I take this opportunity of
congratulating you, not only on your selection but
also on the magnificant victory achieved with the
Welsh 'B' side on Saturday last.

I personally was delighted that you have at last
received in part, the recognition you deserve, lets
hope that you go on to gain even greater honours.
It seems that things have worked out in the end.

Good Luck

Yours sincerely,

Alun J. Priday
Hon.Secretary.

*I hope your Missus has forgiven me at least!
Happy Christmas!*

Almost five years to the day since I had been banned by Cardiff RFC, they
sent me this lovely letter of congratulations after I'd led Wales B to a historic
victory in France.

My ultimate ambition achieved at last. Winning my first cap and leading the team as captain of Wales, against Ireland in Dublin, 1984.

Giving away a penalty against France during my second game at the old National Stadium. The great Jean-Pierre Rives (right) acknowledged that they were fortunate to win that match.

Leading Wales to victory against England at Twickenham in 1984.

The Barbarians team that played against Australia in the final game of their Grand Slam tour of 1984.

A gathering of all the surviving Welsh captains, during the 1999 World Cup.

Me and Maew and some of the teachers from her school. The very same teachers that came to the airport to support Maew when I first arrived in Thailand. They all support Wales now!

It was great to catch-up with Gareth Edwards during the Hong Kong Sevens in 2009.

With Maew's daughter Fai during her school's awards ceremony. She was their top pupil that year. A very proud moment for everyone.

Me and Tim Baggot in Patpong, Bangkok.

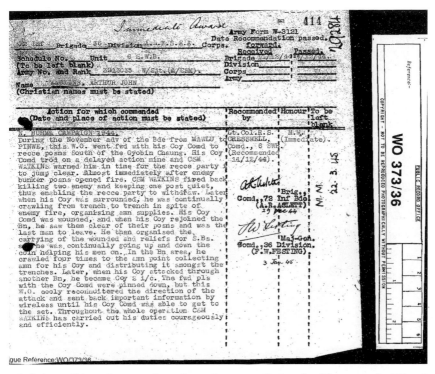

*Immediate Award*

414

Army Form W-3121

72 Inf Brigade 36 Division A.L.F.S.E.A. Corps.

Date Recommendation passed.
forward.
Received. Passed.
Brigade 14/12/44 14/12/44
Division
Corps
Army

Schedule No. Unit 6 S.W.B.
(To be left blank)
Army No. and Rank 3913035 W/Sjt.(A/CSM)

Name WATKINS, ARTHUR JOHN
(Christian names must be stated)

| Action for which commended (Date and place of action must be stated) | Recommended by | Honour | To be left blank |
|---|---|---|---|
| N. BURMA CAMPAIGN 1944. During the November adv of the Bde from MAWLU to PINWE, this W.O. went fwd with his Coy Comd to recce posns South of the Gyobin Chaung. His Coy Comd trod on a delayed action mine and CSM WATKINS warned him in time for the recce party to jump clear. Almost immediately after enemy bunker posns opened fire. CSM WATKINS fired back killing two enemy and keeping one post quiet, thus enabling the recce party to withdraw. Later when his Coy was surrounded, he was continually crawling from trench to trench in spite of enemy fire, organising amn supplies. His Coy Comd was wounded, and when his Coy rejoined the Bn, he saw them clear of their posns and was the last man to leave. He then organised the carrying of the wounded and reliefs for S.Bs. and he was continually going up and down the coln helping his men on. In the Bn area, he crawled four times to the amn point collecting amn for his Coy and distributing it amongst the trenches. Later, when his Coy attacked through another Bn, he became Coy 2 i/c. The fwd pls with the Coy Comd were pinned down, but this W.O. cooly reconnoitered the direction of the attack and sent back important information by wireless until his Coy Comd was able to get to the set. Throughout the whole operation CSM WATKINS has carried out his duties courageously and efficiently. | Lt.Col.R.S. CRESSWELL, Comd., 6 SWB. (Recommended 14/12/44). Comd., 72 Inf Bde (A.R.ASLETT). 29 Dec 44 Comd., 36 Division. (F.W.FESTING). 3 Jan 45 | M.M. (Immediate). | |

I didn't really realise just how big a hero my father had been in the War. I only discovered this after he had passed away.

Me and Maew meet Gareth Bale at the St David's Hotel, Cardiff in November 2013 (thanks to Les Miles).

On one of my trips back to Wales with Roger Powell, Charlie Faulkner and Paul Turner. We're still great friends after all these years.

With Trevor, Tim, Jason ,Me and Huw at the Hong Kong Sevens in 2011. These are some of the guys responsible for persuading me to write this book!

That was a lovely touch about a very memorable day.

Even though we had a great win, the way we, and especially our wives or girlfriends, got treated on that weekend by the WRU beggared belief. First off, our partners weren't allowed to travel up with us on the bus to London. They had to go by train. I can see some logic in that, or at least I could if the other two buses which left Cardiff on that Friday morning hadn't been full of WRU members, and their wives, plus their hangers on, and their pets. I'm sure a Committeeman's dead grandmother in a coffin had a seat by the driver! Ok, I exaggerate ever so slightly, but that's how it felt. Again, we and our wives were treated as second class citizens.

In the evening after the game, while the committee and their wives, along with the dead grandmother, basked in their glory during a huge formal dinner, our wives sat in a pub opposite the hotel waiting for us to join them.

The whole episode made me so angry and upset. They were taking the piss out of us. We sat there, spread out on different tables surrounded by people we didn't know, while our wives weren't even allowed in.

Terry and I finished our food as quick as we could and rushed off to meet our better halves for a few drinks. Later on, we had to sneak them back into our hotel as if they were groupies or prostitutes.

Our wives slept in our beds, while Terry and I kipped on the floor. In the morning, at breakfast, all the English players like Rob Andrew were there with their wives, whilst ours were hiding in the room, waiting for us to pinch the odd piece of toast for them.

When we were leaving, I tried to at least get our wives a lift back to Wales on our bus, one of three hired by the WRU for the players and the committeemen. I was told, in no uncertain terms, that ours was a player-only bus and if I didn't like it, I could find my own way back to Wales. In the end I paid for a taxi to take our wives to the railway station for the train back home. I'm ashamed now that I didn't tell the WRU to stick their bus where the sun doesn't shine, and travel back with my wife on the train to Wales.

My last game for my country took place a few months later, against the all-conquering Australians. A few days before the match Ray Williams, the secretary of the WRU called me to one side after training. 'Hey Spikey, what's it like to be captain of the scruffiest side in Europe?'

I thought he was joking or drunk. He asked again.

'What you on about?' I replied.

He nodded towards the boys sat eating their food. They were mostly dressed in jeans or track suit bottoms and tee-shirts. It wasn't like it is today, where they have sponsored kits for every occasion.

'Well Ray, if you bought us a uniform we'd wear it!'

'They could wear their club blazers.' He said.

'Come on Ray, you want us to turn out for our country wearing our Neath, Swansea or Cardiff club blazers that's not going to help team unity is it?'

He shook his head and walked away as if I'd said something wrong but it wasn't the players fault, and it certainly wasn't my fault that we didn't have proper blazers and kit to wear. Why lay the blame at our feet? Surely, it was their responsibility to kit us out. In my time with the squad, they gave us nothing at all. I didn't even get a Welsh blazer.

I remember in the late 70's the team was sponsored by Adidas and I was given a pair of rugby boots but even that was hard work. I had to sign my soul away to the devil in triplicate, and when I got home the boots didn't fit. So rather than take them back, I took them to a shop in Blackwood. I asked the owner, a good mate, if I could change them.

'Of course, Spikey.' He went out the back and came back in, grinning. 'I got bad news. I can't change them, because they are seconds.'

I couldn't believe it. Even the boots they gave us had something wrong with them. To piss them off, I bought a pair of Patrick boots instead.

Like me, Dai Bishop had been described as a colourful character both off and on the field. One of the best scrum-halves in Wales, maybe the best in the Europe and like me, due to his off-the-field antics, he too had been passed over more times than the houses on the flight path above Heathrow runway.

Everyone, other than the selectors, wanted him to represent our country. Pontypool were the most powerful and successful team of that era. They were basically eight, man-eating forwards with Bish behind them, pulling all the strings. They didn't need, and often, didn't use any of the other backs who sometimes appeared to be there to make up the numbers.

So finally, with Terry gone up North and other scrum-halves struggling with form, Bish got the nod. Apparently, a few bizarre rumours about Bish circulated around Australia at the time. Even the Aussie newspapers printed the story that Dai Bishop was to be released from jail the morning of the game just to play for Wales. I could picture a scene from some American jail movie. The cell door slowly opens, and out of the mist appears some muscle bound, bald-headed lunatic, covered in tattoos, with only one eyebrow and carrying a rugby ball.

'Bish, your country needs you.'

It was all rubbish, but it increased the viewing figures back in Oz I guess. Funnily enough, years later, I was talking to the Australian scrum-half, Nick Farr-Jones about the game. He told me that because he'd heard so much about Bishop's reputation he had decided to have a skinhead, just to make himself look a little harder for the game. The best bit was, his wife saw his new cropped skinhead hairstyle on TV while watching the match and apparently gave him a right royal bollocking when he phoned home.

The Aussies had lost a few of the mid-week games. Cardiff, Ulster, Llanelli, and the South of Scotland had all taken the scalps of the gold and green. Yet when it came to the test matches, no one could live with them. Wins against England and Ireland meant they only had us and the Scots to beat to become the first ever Australian side to do the four home nations Grand Slam. Their team was packed full of established, and up-and-coming, superstars. The likes of David Campese, Nick Farr-Jones, Andrew Slack the Captain, Michael Lynagh, Simon Poidevin and Mark Ella.

The night before the game we were holed up in the Angel Hotel in Cardiff city centre and I called a meeting of senior players. I was wondering if this should be my last game for Wales, and if so I wanted to go out with a win and a bang. So, with Eddie, and Pickering, 'Coffee Table Arse' Ackerman, Norster and a few others, we began formalizing a game plan.

After about 30 minutes of deep conversation, Butler suggested we ordered a few sandwiches and some coffees. I phoned down to room service and thought no more of it. We carried on with our discussion on how to win the game. The food and drink arrived.

By the time we finished our meeting, we all had fire in our bellies. I couldn't wait for the game. The day itself, couldn't have been worse. It was cold, muddy and rained like there was no tomorrow. Maybe the bad weather was a blessing in disguise. Some of the stuff the Aussies did on the field, even in those conditions, was just incredible. Campese dazzled everyone with his pace and his cheek. Their angles of running and ball skills and confidence were amazing.

Halfway through the second half, we suffered the biggest humiliation for a pack of forwards. On their ball, but on our five metre line, they called out 'eight man scrum' and then pushed us over our line to score a try. I hung my head in shame.

We came back at them and it was good to see Bish getting a well-earned try. He acrobatically leapt through the air, juggling with the wet ball before touching down. After that the Aussies ran away with it. We ended up losing 28-9, which was a good thumping in anyone's book.

Our humiliation didn't stop there. At the after-match dinner, Andrew Slack, their captain, made a heart-warming speech and thanked us for a really hard game. He then called me up and presented me a big plaque in commemoration of their British tour. It looked beautiful. Then he handed over 21 blazer pins and 21 ties for all our squad, before sitting down. I stood there, knowing full well we had no plaque, no blazer pins and no ties to give them. The checklist committeeman had fouled-up again.

I had to think on my feet. I thanked Andrew and his team on their performance, and their big win and hoped they continued the following weekend and sealed their first ever Grand Slam. Then I apologised because I didn't have anything to give them. 'Someone in the Welsh Rugby Union forgot,' I blurted out. 'I feel so embarrassed. But you must forgive us, because you know how much it cost to build our new stadium, so we are strapped for cash at this moment.'

All the hot-shots in their dickie bows, puffing on their expensive cigars, squirmed in their seats. I went off on one and there was no stopping me this time. I could see all the players grinning from ear to ear. Suddenly, someone pulled my sleeve and handed me an old crumpled-up Welsh tie, which looked like it had egg stains all down the front.

'Oh, here you are Andrew, as if by magic, this tie has

suddenly appeared. It's made out of polyester; its top class.' Laughter filled the room from certain quarters. Silence from others. I continued, 'I believe you are here for another 30 days, so if you wear this tie tomorrow and then start giving it to the rest of the team in alphabetical order, you should all have had a little go of it by the time you go back home.' I handed it over and sat down.

All the Australians, to a man, stood up and started applauding. Lots of my team did the same.

After it was over, Ray Williams came storming up to me. 'There was no need for that. You really embarrassed us.'

I could feel the colour draining from my cheeks and the mist coming down. This time Terry wasn't there to whisper, 'Michael John, leave it' in my ear.

I turned and stared at Ray. 'Let's get this right....I embarrassed you...I embarrassed you. Hang on just a minute. You fucking embarrassed me. I was the one standing up with only my dick in my hand. Now piss off.'

The worse thing about the whole shambles was they had been too stubborn to admit they had screwed-up; not to me and not to the players. I don't mind a person messing up, that's life, but be man enough to come clean when it happens.

If the fiasco over the gifts hadn't made my mind up about quitting, a letter I received a few days later from them, not only put a top hat on it, it took it to the bloody theatre as well. I opened the letter to find the WRU had billed me £38 for the coffee and sandwiches I'd ordered for the team meeting in my room on the Friday night. I stared at it in disbelief. It wasn't like I had watched £38 worth of blue movies or had ordered a bottle of champagne.

I called Ray up. 'Listen, about this letter. That night I called a team meeting, a serious players meeting. We really wanted to give them a game.'

'No you can't do that,' he flatly replied, 'you aren't allowed.'

'I'm not allowed,' I yelled back, 'I am the Captain of the team, not some school kid on a trip to Barry Island. We're representing our country. It was a few ham sandwiches and some hot drinks. It wasn't even beer.'

I was warned to pay it or else.

I ripped the letter up. I earned £100 a week and they wanted me to hand over almost half of my weekly wage for something I was doing for them, and my country. It was too funny to be laughable. If I had been a multi-millionaire, I still wouldn't have paid it on principle. While we were having a meeting discussing tactics, they were all down in the bar, probably smoking top class cigars and sipping cognac. There had been a full house at the Arms Park that day, plus with TV rights and all the rest of the jazz, they were telling me, they couldn't afford thirty-eight bloody quid....I ask you!!!?

Today, it would be like asking Sam Warburton for half his weekly wages to cover the refreshments bill whilst holding a team meeting. It just wouldn't happen!

I was sick of being treated like a kid so I refused to pay it. They sent solicitor's letter after solicitor's letter, until they finally gave up.

To say I was pissed off with the pettiness of the WRU and their truly unprofessional approach would be an understatement. It seemed like I was fighting a constant battle against them. Even when claiming expenses, they always made you feel as if you were ripping them off. I'd put in 25 miles to travel to Cardiff from my home. They would check it. I think they used to pay someone to drive from door to door just to make sure we weren't pulling a fast one. They came back to me and said it wasn't 25 miles and they would only allow for 18 and a half miles. As if the allowance for that extra 6 and a half miles would cover the income I lost as a result of playing for Wales.

I didn't respect the WRU committee to the same degree that they clearly didn't respect me. In my opinion they were a bunch of amateurs. The only difference I see today since everything has gone professional is that the WRU us now run by a bunch of professionals but the mentality is still the same.

I once read an article which made me laugh out loud. The article said, 'You mention the name Spikey Watkins in the Welsh Rugby Union committee box and 50% of them will say, "What a character!" and the other 50% of them will spit out their gin and tonics'.

That is exactly how divided they were over me. In my opinion, many of them just jumped on the anti-Spikey bandwagon. Often there was no proof to the hearsay about me. It was just people saying, 'Oh I heard Spikey was up to this and that last week.' The way it was made out, I had been the mastermind behind the Great Train Robbery, even though I was only twelve when it happened. Stories got exaggerated; but the powers-that-be believed every word and probably added a few more paragraphs on themselves. They seemed to enjoy classing me as a nutter. Unfortunately, if people wanted to see my worst side I would give it to them, ten fold. If they pulled my tail, I wouldn't hold back. That was one of my problems.

In the end, even though I had been promised the Captaincy for at least another year, I decided to call it a day. I loved being Captain of my country, but I hated all the petty politics and falseness surrounding it. I hated the way they treated us like we were in a parent/child relationship.

Nevertheless, that wasn't the primary reason. Financially, I was on the bones of my arse. My Dad and I weren't talking, which meant I wasn't working and I didn't have a cheque coming through the door. Everyone kept telling me how upset my father was and how I'd let him down but I was the one not earning any money. The pressure on me, on and off the field, was immense. They didn't know the half of it! It felt like I had won the lottery being captain of Wales, but the cheque never fell through the letterbox.

There was no sponsorship, or cosy little office jobs, coming my way. I thought that, being captain, someone would offer me a job, but I had nothing. If I had been paid I reckon I would still be booting players in the chops until I was 93.

After a match was over and the press conference done, and the Sunday papers read the next morning, that was it. Come Monday, reality kicked back in and I was skint. My family suffered. There were arguments at home about me going training when my wife thought I should be out finding a job.

I wonder, if it all reverted back to those amateur days, would the players of today do it for nothing? Would they do it for the love of the game, a few beers and a sing song after?

I never recovered financially. There was only so long I could dip into our savings, so after the Australian match, I listened to my bank manager and tried to get a proper, paying, day job.

On the day I retired from international rugby, I told the newspapers, instead of the WRU. I didn't see anything wrong in that. They had done the same to me over the years. When I was dropped or even when I had been selected, I would find out by reading the paper, not by a phone call. I gave them back some of their own medicine.

To prove my point, no one from the Union ever rang to ask me why I had quit. In all probability it was because often the truth hurts.

# 10

# Dirty Tricks and Cocktail Sticks

*"On the field Spikey always was a hard, physical player with no punches pulled whether he played for or against and on times had to have the last word even to the referee. He knew the laws and also knew how to break them and if he got away with it he would run away and smile at you. I was lucky I always got on well with him, not like some referees. Off the field after a game he was not shy to come and talk and explain what he thought of the game or my refereeing and to clarify what had happened during the game. What a leader and motivator this man was."*

**Les Peard**
**International Referee**

Some people have a fear of dying, or flying, or getting trapped in a broken-down lift with a murderer. But my biggest fear is far worse than all of those put together.

My biggest fear, which often wakes me up in a cold sweat, was that one day I'd transform into, a committeeman! I remember a film about a man who metamorphosed into a beetle. The difference was instead of shedding my skin and replacing it with insect skin, in my dream, I found myself in a cheap, polyester blazer, a club tie with food stains on it, slacks, slip-on shoes, white socks and a beer belly. In my nightmare, my bed was surrounded by an army of committeemen marching after me like zombies, clutching free beer tokens. The nearer my full retirement loomed, the more frightening my recurring dream became.

I've been asked many times why, as a leader on and off field, I had such an issue with people in authority. I didn't think I had a problem with authority figures, well only a certain few! There were many I got on exceptionally well with, the guys who ran Crawshays rugby are a fine example, but I must be on equal terms with them on a personal level. It's all a matter of giving and receiving respect. How can you respect someone who has been put in a position of power and trust when you know they, to put it mildly, aren't up to the role? Too many Welsh Rugby Union officials have crawled and licked boots to get where they are. They are yes-men, the sort of people who would stab you in the back but say nothing to your face! I won't be sycophantic to anyone I don't like. I would rather just not talk to them.

One of the reasons I wanted to lead, was that I didn't want to be led by people like that. I wasn't afraid to stand and fall by my decisions, good or bad, right or wrong. I think my father, in an odd sort of way, made me stand on my own two feet and survive. Like father like son. From his army days he had to survive or die! As I got older I saw my father coming out in me on lots of occasions. He never suffered fools, as I don't.

I have had to learn to survive from an early age. Many times these so-called authority figures tried to beat me down, but it never worked, which I believe frustrated them to hell. Charlie used to say, when I got into trouble and came out the other end, 'Spike can survive where a rat won't.'

I don't think he was far wrong.

So I laughed loudly when people asked me if I was going to

join the committee at Newport when I retired. I would rather have hot pins stuck in my eyes and the committee at Newport would probably rather have hot pins stuck in their eyes than see me join their ranks. Some joker suggested I should become a referee but that was definitely never going to happen. During my career, and even beyond it, I developed a love/hate relationship with referees; probably more hate than love if I am honest. I guess I gave more refs more sleepless nights than all the other players put together.

'The son of Satan,' one referee once called me.

For my part, I thought Clive Norling was the finest and definitely one of the most flamboyant hanging judges on the circuit. A proper dictatorial bastard, but a fair dictatorial bastard all the same. He certainly had his quirks and often, just like the WRU, he treated players like school kids.

Down the years, Clive and I had what I would call a strained relationship, a bit like an old married couple, but with him definitely wearing the trousers. I think he liked me really, but there were occasions when I'm sure if he'd had a gun he wouldn't have thought twice about blowing my head clean off.

In one game for Newport, I must have done something to wind him up big style. He kept penalising me and we were losing badly as well, so I wasn't in the best of moods. While a player lay on the ground receiving treatment, nothing to do with me I must add, I ambled up to Clive.

'Oh Clive.'

'Get away, Spike,'

'Clive, mun.'

'Go away I said.'

I offered him a drink from the water bottle. 'Look Clive,' I quickly added, 'can I ask you a question?'

He turned to face me, 'What?'

'Clive, what would you do if I called you a cunt?'

With complete horror on his face, he replied, 'I would send you off, Spikey.'

The injured player got up and the game continued. The next break in play, I sided-up to him again.

'Clive.'

'What now, Spike?'

'Can I ask you another question?'

He nodded his head. 'What is it?'

'What would you do if I thought you were a cunt?'

He looked at me, confusion written all over his face. 'Well I couldn't do anything if you just thought it, could I?'

'Well, Clive, I think you're a cunt.'

He glared at me, before bursting out laughing. It must have worked because, he stopped penalising me and we won the game!

As a Captain, I believed one of my roles was to know exactly how to play the ref. To do this I needed to get close to them and develop a rapport, so I knew what we could get away with. There was a skill and an art to it and I often took it to the limit. More often than not, I could see the dread on their faces when I appeared by their side.

'You're having a good game ref.'

'Get away from me Spikey, get away.'

'I'm only telling you. You are doing well.'

'Get away. I know what you are trying to do. Now go before I penalise you.'

'For what?'

'You know what.'

If we were playing away, the entire home crowd would be spitting feathers. I really was the baddie from the pantomime, and I liked it. 'Watkins, get away from the ref, you are trying to influence him.' The fans would be going bonkers.

'Oh no, I'm not.'

'Oh yes you are...leave him alone.'

'Oh no, I'm not.'

'Oh yes you are,' the referee would hiss, 'now go away.'

Some referees would head me off at the pass. They often called me to one side before the start of the game. 'Look Spikey who's refereeing the game today?'

'You are of course, ref.'

'Well leave me do it.'

'I always do, ref'

'Don't push it Spike, or you will be having an early bath, now go away.'

I did have a lot of respect for some of them. It was a tough gig. In those days they really needed eyes in the back of their heads. In fact they needed eyes right around their heads. There would be violence and skullduggery all over the field and it was left to them to sort it out. The ref was a lone figure and they didn't have neutral linesmen to help them out. Most of the time the lines were run by biased, one-eyed committeemen, who were the worst cheats this side of the Severn Bridge.

Then again, one game down in Swansea, I did something which caught Clive out, and he never forgave me for it for the rest of his refereeing career.

It was a big televised cup game. Going into the last five minutes we were losing by two points and we had a lineout near their line. We'd been working on an 'underhand' set move in training. The idea was that while the ref stood at the back of the lineout, I'd throw the ball in to the middle. Then I would grab my opposite hooker and drag him into the lineout, leaving the touch line unguarded. Our player carrying the ball would peel around the front, run into the space vacated by their hooker, and hopefully score a try.

So with time ticking away, I called the move and it worked

**160**

a treat. While their hooker was trying to get free by punching me, the team executed the move perfectly and we scored a try in the corner to seal the win.

There was absolute pandemonium in the ground.

Their players went nuts.

Their committee went nuts.

Their crowd went nuts.

The ball boy went nuts.

We went nuts because we were winning.

With all this going on, Norling hadn't seen anything wrong. He stood behind the try line, while all the home fans screamed at him. He knew something had happened but didn't know what.

He glared at me. I grinned back. He called me towards him.

'What happened, Spike?'

'What?'

'Don't give me "What"? What did you do?' He said in his full headmaster's voice.

'Nothing Clive, honest, cross my arse and hope to die.'

I ran off. We won the game.

Obviously, he saw the replay the next day on TV and like an elephant, wearing shorts and holding a silver whistle, he didn't forget. During our next game together, he may as well have sent me off before I ran out on the pitch as he penalised me even if I was nowhere near the ball. I think he even gave me a warning for winning the toss. I could easily have been in the Guinness Book of Records for giving away the most penalties in one match. Not surprisingly, we lost the match heavily. Everyone blamed me.

Although referees have a tough job, a sense of humour and a bit of commonsense wouldn't go amiss at times. In my day, it would probably have made their job a little easier. Yet some referees just didn't have a clue how to help themselves.

When I retired, Charlie and I were asked to play in a charity game in Caerphilly for the opening of their new club house. I was touching 45 by then and Charlie must have been at least 79 years old. Ok, maybe 76. By this time I hadn't played serious rugby for almost 10 years.

Our team was a mixture of old and young players and I had agreed to play with the understanding it would be a bit of fun with a little rugby breaking out now and again. The referee, Gwyn Bowden, marched onto the field as if he was in charge of the World Cup final, ball under his arm and his whistle shining as though he'd been up all night polishing it. I could tell, he was the type who didn't have a funny bone in his body.

From the kick-off, the ref wanted to show he was the boss. He gave penalty after penalty, often for small, stupid offences. It was hard enough playing in a game when I hadn't played for years, never mind a full-blooded match, but I didn't have to be there. There was no money for doing it. It was just a charity fun thing and I didn't want to get an injury.

I said, 'Come on ref, lighten up a bit. We are here to entertain the crowd, not bore them to death.'

'Shut up and play the game,' he grunted.

This went on and on. After about twenty minutes I'd had enough. When the ball went into touch, I sat on it and started having a *craic* with some people in the crowd. 'Well, no wonder Welsh Rugby is in the state it is in, with people like him running the show.' I said.

'Get on with the game.' The ref stormed over to me.

'I'm talking to the crowd.'

He stood right in my face. 'Carry on with the game.'

'I'm talking.'

'Carry on or I'll send you off.'

'For what?'

He seemed flustered, 'For...for...for not carrying on with the game.'

'It's a charity match.' The crowd started laughing. I turned to them 'See what I mean.'

Trying to get the ball off me, he bellowed, 'Right, I'm sending you off.'

'Look ref; don't be stupid, this is a bit of fun.'

'Off!'

'Look.'

'Off.'

That was it, the mist came down. 'Look mate, you don't need to send me off, I'm going.' I grabbed out at his jersey, trying to stick the ball up his shirt. 'Keep your fucking ball.'

With the crowd cheering and clapping I stormed off. I got showered and drove home. I was tamping but also more than happy I didn't have anything to do with that game, or anything to do with rugby in general.

A week later another letter fell through my letterbox from the WRU. The first thing I thought was, 'not another demand for £38 for the Angel Hotel's sandwiches and drinks'. Then I read it. *'It has been brought to our attention you were sent off in a game between Caerphilly and an invitation team.'*

I thought, what the hell are they on about now. It had been a charity thing, a bit of fun. I continued reading. *'You can appeal if you want in person or if you don't your case will be dealt with by a five man committee next week.'*

I really didn't know if I should have laughed or cried. Of all the things going on in the world, I get a letter like this but I knew one thing. I wasn't going to miss my hearing even if I had to crawl there on my hands and knees.

I turned up in Cardiff and as I entered the room, the five members of the WRU sat around the table, handing out black hats like the scene in Blackadder. In the corner, I imagined a huge, bare-chested man in a mask, stood holding an axe!

I sat down.

'Are you Michael John Watkins?' one of them asked me.

'Course I am....you all know me.'

'Just answer the questions.' I felt like I was in a Spanish jail, being interviewed for smuggling drugs.

They repeated the question.

'No,' I wanted to say, 'I'm Donald sodding Duck.' But I didn't, 'YES I am Michael John Watkins.'

One of them wrote it down in the minutes.

'Did you on such and such a date touch a referee?'

I laughed. They made me sound like a paedophile, or a ref-o-phile or a paed-o-ref. 'I tried to put the ball up his jumper, if you must know.' I said.

'Do you think that was wrong?' one of the others chipped in.

'Not really, no.'

'Do you regret what you did?'

I could see where this was heading. With me going straight into a brick wall, head first without a seat belt on. 'Tell you what I do regret,' I whispered. They automatically leant in closer to me. 'I regret now that I didn't just ram the ball up his fucking arse.'

There wasn't a smile on any of their faces. I think if they could have sentenced me to be beheaded they would have. The imaginary man in the mask, holding the axe, inched forward.

I didn't want to listen to this anymore. It was utter nonsense of the highest order. When walking out, I turned back. 'By the way,' I said calmly, 'I know where you lot sell your international tickets at inflated prices.'

I could hear a pin drop.

'No you don't. No you don't,' one of them piped up.

'I know exactly where you sell them.'

I stormed out and slammed the door.

The next day on the front page of the Western Mail newspaper, it stated in black and white, 'Ex-rugby Captain gets 36 week ban.' There could have been an earthquake in India, a train crash in Italy, even if Elvis had been found living on an island with Lord Lucan and Shergar, it was me who had made the front pages yet again.

The crazy thing was, they banned me for 36 weeks even though I had no intention of ever playing again. It made no difference to me at all. It was like something from Catch 22; a totally meaningless ban. What a bunch of stupid idiots. I imagined them patting each other on the back, 'We've had him this time.'

I think that ban summed up the madness and politics throughout rugby in those days. When I retired from being captain of Wales, I got invited to be a guest on the BBC quiz show, A Question of Sport, which was quite a big honour. It was one of the most popular shows on TV.

I sat on Emlyn Hughes' team along with Sam Torrance. The captain of the other team was English rugby legend Billy Beaumont with boxing icon Barry McGuigan and tennis star Annabel Croft. I travelled up to Manchester to do the show on a Sunday night, stayed at a hotel and travelled home on the Monday. A week later, I received another letter from the WRU. It started in typical fashion, *'It's been brought to our attention..... you have been on 'A Question of Sport.'* I came to the conclusion they must have had thousands of pre-written letters printed on headed paper starting with the words. *It has been brought to our attention.* Most of them addressed to me.

The letter stated, *'We know the fee is around £200 to £300 and if you keep the money you will be classed as a professional and not allowed to play again. We suggest you give the money to the WRU Charitable Trust.'*

I thought 'you cheeky bastards'. When you think of how much footballers and rugby players get paid today, I could have worked a shift in my truck and earned some of that. As far as I was concerned I wasn't representing my country, I didn't have to do it.

I decided the WRU Charitable Trust would be the last place I would give it. I would rather have given it to the Dublin cat burglar. I didn't even know they had a Trust, never mind what its purpose was. I got advice from Newport, my club. They concluded I couldn't keep it or I would be struck down with boils and made to live a life in agony and turmoil. In the end I gave it to the Newport Rugby Club tour fund. At least the boys had a beer out of it.

It was a sham. Just like when the 'Not getting paid for playing' scandal broke in Wales in the 1980's. Unknown sources claimed players like me got hundreds of pounds a week stuffed in their rugby boots by their clubs. Believe it or not, I checked my boots regularly after each match and there was never anything in there. Cardiff and Newport treated me fairly, but no money ever went from hand to boot.

Along with many other players, I received a boot money letter from the WRU. They demanded to know if I had received money for playing. My reply back to them, simply stated, 'I'm still waiting for my carrot to arrive.'

I never heard back.

Before I finally retired from the sport I loved, I squeezed in a few more memorable moments.

One I remember well was the day, or more importantly the night, I played for a RFU 'World XV' against England to celebrate Twickenham's 75th anniversary. Our team read like the Who's Who of Rugby. Danny Gerber, Errol Tobias and Rob Louw of

South Africa, plus a few old Welsh colleagues in the shape of Rob Ackerman, Ikey Stephens and Terry Holmes. England fielded a half decent side as well, with the likes of Stuart Barnes, Rory Underwood, Clive Woodwood and the captain, John Scott

We won quite convincingly, 27 points to 10, without breaking into too much of a sweat or needing to throw any punches, well, not too many punches!

The night after the game, we stayed at the Hilton Hotel in the centre of London. My room mate was the massive 6 foot 7, second row forward, Rudi Visagie from South Africa. He was such a giant of a man that when he stood by the window he blocked out the sun! Dressed up in his Springbok blazer, he looked the business. A real good looking man with a huge 1970's style dodgy moustache on him.

At the big post-match banquet in the Hilton we sat through the same old boring nonsense of endless speech after endless speech by the blazer and tie brigade. Then, one by one, the players started to disappear.

I thought I'd better stay, or I'd get in trouble. In the end, I couldn't stick it anymore and whispered to Rudi for us to get out of there. It was easy for me to blend in with the waiters while making my escape, not so easy for a man the same size as a Canadian Oak Tree. But he made it.

Underneath the hotel was a posh cocktail bar, Trader Vic's. I had a feeling where everyone would be and I was right. They were all sat in the corner, with an array of different cocktail in front of them.

As I walked in, Ikey Stephens shouted across, 'Hey Scotty.... how are you?'

Then someone else did the same.

At first I didn't cotton on, or Scotton on, why they were all calling me John Scott, the English captain.

The head waiter came rushing over, 'Hello Mister Scott, I hope its ok, but your players have been booking drinks to your room.'

In the background, Terry stood up and gave me the old nod and a wink.

With a straight face, I replied, 'How much have they booked?'

'Oh, Mister Scott it's over £200.' He looked like he was about to burst into tears. 'Oh,' I slowly shook my head, 'well, that's not too bad, not bad at all. I tell you what, take it up to about five or six hundred...and let me know, but,' I added, 'remember one thing.' Everyone looked at me, 'no cigars, they can't have any cigars. And by the way, get everyone in the bar including your staff a drink.'

'Thank you sir, thank you.' He crawled away.

'Spikey,' Rudi stood next to me, a confused look on his face, 'what are you doing?'

'Don't worry Rudi...it will be ok.'

For the next 45 minutes, everything went cocktail crazy. Weird drinks appeared on every table. The boys just started making up their own cocktails and giving them names such as 'The Drop-Goal', 'The Terry Holmes', and 'The All Committeemen Are a Bunch of Bastards.' That was my favourite!

Within the hour, the main waiter sidled back. 'Mister Scott, the bill is up to £750 now. I'm so sorry, I didn't realise.'

'What?' I bellowed, 'well if that's the case, take it up to a grand and I'll review the situation after that.'

I started showing off and buying any girl who walked into the bar whatever they wanted.

'Mister Scott it's a thousand pounds now....' Even before he finished his sentence, I piped up, 'Take it to £1500.' A streak of wickedness in Nike trainers raced through my body. I didn't even think of what was going to happen.

In the end, the bill came to just over £1,600. A lot of money even today, and an awful lot of dosh in those days for some coloured water with gin in it. As he handed me the bill to sign, all the players made a dash for it like the Von Trapp family in the Sound of Music. All except for Rudi, the loyal Free State player. He stood by my side.

I casually took the receipt off the waiter and signed John's name. I knew how John did his signature so that was easy.

'What is your room number, Mister Scott?' he asked.

Now I was stuck. I hadn't got a clue. First number which sprang into my mind was room 365.

'Thanks sir.'

As we were walking away, he suddenly said, 'Hang on, there's no 365 in the hotel.'

Grabbing Rudi, we both did a runner, up the steps, and hopped into the first taxi we could find.

We had got away with the great cocktail scam of Old London Town.

Rudi turned to me and asked, 'Spikey, will you take me to the place where all the lights are. The place I've seen on the television.'

He meant Piccadilly, so of course we ended up in the middle of Soho. Gangs of pissed up girls tried their best to grab the good looking rugby player who looked like Magnum PI. However hard I tried, none of them fancied grabbing me.

'Spikey I don't like it here...take me back to the hotel,' he grimaced.

We got back about one in the morning. It was all quiet on the Hilton front.

Unaware to us, security had been tipped off to look out for a Welsh person calling himself John Scott and a huge South African dressed to the nines. Even if they had been the dullest people in the entire world, they couldn't have missed us. We must have looked like Giant Haystacks and one of the Krankies waddling in to the foyer, drunk.

They all turned and stared at us.

Suddenly, the waiter and the manager appeared like genies from a bottle. The waiter identified me as the cocktail con-man. They demanded I paid the bill immediately or they would call the police.

I had to think fast. 'No, I'm a guest of the RFU.' I said, 'Now go and get Derek Morgan right now.' I knew Derek very well. He was the top dog in the RFU.

They sent someone to get him out of bed. He came down in his dressing gown and slippers, his hair all sticking up. He took one look at me and said, 'What have you done now, Spikey?'

If I had a penny for every time someone said that to me, I could have paid John Scott's cocktail bar bill and still had the taxi fare back home to Wales.

I did what I did best. I quickly turned defence into all out attack. 'Bloody hell Derek.....you guys are exactly like the Welsh Rugby Union's bunch of bastards. We've come up here, entertaining thousands of fans, we haven't been paid, in fact, I lost money for not working and now you want me to pay a little bar bill.'

I'm not sure if he was too tired or too angry to argue. 'Ok, Spikey....just, just...just go.'

I didn't expect him to give in so easily, 'Derek you are worse than those Welsh tossers....much worse.'

'Spikey....I'll sort it...just go.'

Still talking, Rudi dragged me off to bed.

And that was the last I heard of the bill. On saying that, I didn't get picked to play for them again either.

On the same trip to South Africa, where I organised the raffle with a difference for the committeeman's wife and whacked a crocodile over the head with a seven iron, I woke up one sunny morning, to find something odd wandering around my room. Over the years I've found my fair share of odd things wandering around my room. Normally, some old tart looking for her underwear or her teeth or both! But even I was shocked when to see a big, hairy, Orang-utan swinging on the light shade. The first thing I thought was, 'Bloody hell, that lager must have been strong last night.'

It must have climbed in through my bedroom window. I did think maybe Steve Fenwick had followed me over there and finally got revenge for the Koala bear incident.

I lay there, naked and afraid to move, and then tried to shoo it out of the room but it went for me! It was unbelievable; I felt like Charlton Heston in the blue version of Planet of the Apes. I opened the bedroom door to call for help, but the creature raced straight out past me and down the corridor. Two old cleaning ladies screamed. The ape then, apparently, ran amok through the hotel. I went back to bed.

I didn't play much more rugby after that trip. Nothing to do with the Orang-utan, it was just that I had got to the stage where I wasn't enjoying it anymore. I continued with Charlie Faulkner RFC until the end of the 1986/87 season and it proved to be a season of breaking records. We had the most wins, the highest number of points scored, the most tries and we finished the season runners-up in the merit table. Not a bad way of signing out. That was the end of it in my mind. Then for some reason, I played one match for Newbridge at the start of the following season, but got sent off within twenty minutes and thought, 'I can't be arsed with this anymore.' By the way, the ref who sent me packing on that day was Clive 'don't pull the wool over my eyes ever again Spikey' Norling. He definitely had his revenge.

# 11

# High Tailing it Through the Dark Clouds

*"Mike was a world class player, who was one of the game's great leaders and captains. Off the field he is one of life's great characters, who can fill a room with his personality. I got to know Mike when I was a youngster just out of youth rugby as he was a friend of my father. Knowing I played hooker he kindly invited me to train with him at Newport RFC, which proved to be a great experience. I got to learn from one of the best. He is a generous man who is great fun to be around. I'm proud to call him a friend, Mike 'Spikey' Watkins, a true rugby legend!!!"*

**Nigel Meek**
**Pontypool - Wales**

It was a strange emotion when I finally hung up my boots. A feeling that got worse as the weeks progressed. It felt like I'd been driving a car in the fast lane with a gang of my mates all of my life, and then all of a sudden I'd smashed head first into a brick wall.

The sudden emptiness took a lot of getting used to and it meant a huge readjustment to my day-to-day life. I'd played rugby from the age of 12 right up to the age of 35, which is one hell of a long time. I'd also played most of my rugby at a high level. Running out in front of big crowds, that had been either shouting for me to win or baying for my blood, but whatever they were doing, it was still my stage and I was the performer.

It also wasn't just about the 80 minutes out on the field on a Saturday. I so missed the training, the banter in the changing rooms and the end of season tours. I even missed the small things like reading the match reports in the Sunday newspapers. When I played for Newport, I had my own car park space. Then when it was over, my space was passed on to the next generation of players.

My sporting life, as I had known it, began to slip away from me. Rugby had been my drug, my natural high, my daily adrenaline rush. My body had got used to it. Without it I regressed into a state of cold turkey. I suffered like hell from depression for quite a few years. It's hard to explain. A big, black cloud followed me around wherever I went.

I often sat alone in my flat, my mind racing, contemplating all the stuff I could and should have done when I had been playing.

I can understand how other ex-sportsmen and women sink into despair when they hang up their boots or hockey sticks or whatever. It does become a nightmare. Even my favourite old referee, Clive Norling, missed the excitement and buzz so much that he suffered from the same condition.

Many retired sportsmen go straight into coaching but I didn't fancy it, at that time. A few lucky ones, like Jonathan Davies, go on to make a decent living as TV pundits. Sadly, I didn't have BBC executives beating my door down for my words of wisdom.

What did I do? I went drinking so that I could forget about the highs and cope with the lows, and there were lots more low points than highs after I'd stopped. No one sees that part of it. I lost my direction and my purpose in life. To add to my misery, my marriage went the same way as my career, straight into the same brick wall.

After 19 years with Stephanie our marriage started to come to an end, but in all honesty it had been on the cards for a while. It was odd; because we had met so young it was like we were like brother and sister at times. Both of us changed over the years and we were both looking for new things in our lives. We shared a big house together but that was the top and bottom of our relationship. It got to the point where there was no warmth in our lives. Everything between us felt cold and nothing exciting happened anymore.

I know it sounds petty, but a defining moment came when I found out she'd taped over all of my games and TV interviews. Even the VHS tape of me on *A Question of Sport*, which she'd replaced with *Neighbours*! Had she no respect, or not thought of what it meant to me? Or maybe she did!

I'm ashamed to say I started an affair with a girl in my office, but my wife soon found out about it. I was quite relieved really as I didn't like telling all the lies. It's not in my personality. It actually made my nerves bad. We tried to make a fresh go of it but it was never the same after. What put the top hat on it was the night when I heard shouting and stones being thrown at our windows. It was the woman I was having a relationship with. She was outside the house. The commotion woke everyone, including my daughters and the people next door. I didn't want anything to do with that crazy woman, but I knew it was over with my wife from that moment.

I put all my worldly belongings into plastic bin liners and left the house, like a bag-lady. However, we all know what the valleys are like, and soon all the goings on with the ex-Wales captain became a major talking point. My daughters would have nothing to do with me, let alone talk to me. My Mam and Dad were old and they didn't want all the stress. I felt alone.

When Stephanie filed for divorce I contested nothing. I agreed to all my ex-wife's demands so she kept everything in the house, leaving me with not one stick of furniture, only my photos from my rugby days and my international jerseys. She also had the cars but then again, they were no good to me. I couldn't drive because I had been banned.

With my rugby career over and my marriage sliding down the drain, I filled the void by spending most of my days in O'Reillys in the centre of Newport. I even had my own little spot in the corner, where, I would sit necking way too much Diamond White cider and Southern Comfort. It really was a den of iniquity; a much rougher version of the space station bar in Star Wars. All the losers from the town gathered there. Druggies, piss heads, criminals and no hopers. I would look around and snigger and think, 'How bad are these people. Haven't they got anything better to do with their lives?'

Then, after a few weeks I realised, I was one of them. I was a mental-head, a no hoper. Probably, there was someone sitting in their own spot, staring at me and thinking the same thing as I had weeks before.

I then ambled around in life, not going anywhere fast. I started going out with a string of women, but nothing serious. There was one girl I had a bit of a fling with and my God she was so supple, like seven and a half stone of pure, raw, plasticine dressed up in suspenders and not much else! Late one night while sitting in her flat, she whispered in my ear, 'Spikey, you can do anything you want to me.'

Bloody Hell! I thought I already had. Maybe she was thinking of a threesome or dogging up the woods.

'Come on Spikey,' she said, 'there must be something you've always wanted to do.'

My little, old, trusty devil popped up on my shoulder. 'Go on,' it hissed, 'throw it out there. See what she says.'

I turned to face her. 'Ok....I've...always wanted to......wanted to.....shag a girl on the halfway line of Cardiff Arms Park before they knock it down.' I'm not sure if it was a fetish or just plain 'rebellion against the system'.

She looked at me kind of strangely. 'Oh ok. Let's go.'

It was a lovely warm summer's night. We drove into the centre of Cardiff in her sports car at two in the morning. By the light of the moon, arm in arm and giggling like a pair of drunken teenagers, we snaked our way across the field of the Athletic Cub. We clambered over the big gates leading into the National Stadium. This time I made sure there wasn't a rogue spike to fall on.

We sneaked down the tunnel onto the field. In my mind I imagined the stands full of Welshmen, all paying good money to watch me give her one on the halfway line. I walked out with my chest puffed out and my old boy beginning to stand to attention.

The only problem was, I'd forgotten it was pre-season and the grass was a couple of feet high. There were also no markings, so I wasn't sure where the centre spot actually was.

'Well let's just do it here,' she said grabbing me.

'No. It's got to be exactly on the half way line.' God knows why, but I was determined. The idea had been planted in my mind and I wasn't going to take second best.

'Wait there.' I said as I marched away from her towards one of the corners. I bounded diagonally from one corner to the other, leaving a trail in the long grass. I did the same from the opposite corners. Then I walked from behind the middle of the goal posts to the other end. I must have looked like a complete nutcase. It took me about 15 minutes but there was method in my madness.

Where all the lines crossed I assumed was more or less the middle.

I stood there, out of breath. 'Right, get your arse down on there.' I could be such a romantic at times.

Being in the open air added a slice more passion to the occasion. With her legs wrapped around my waist, I pumped away, half of me focused on the job at hand; the other half of me hilariously pictured all the great players who had proudly jogged out on the field in the past. I even thought about that great Barbarian try against the All Blacks. The commentary played over and over in my head. It all added to the excitement.

When my 'whistle' finally blew, and we stood up, there was a complete outline of her arse in the centre. Never mind crop circles. We had just left our very own Arse Circle. I couldn't help but imagine the groundsman in the morning staring at it and then scratching his head and looking up at the sky.

'That was wonderful, do you want to do anything else?' She said with a wicked look on her face.

'Rodney Parade,' I muttered. The little devil on my shoulder bounced up and down in delight.

'What?'

'I want to do it again on the half-way line at Rodney Parade in Newport.'

'Serious.'

'Yeah.'

'When?'

'Now. Tonight.'

She shrugged, 'Ok.'

As a result we quickly left the Arms Park and drove the 20 or so miles to Newport, where we clambered into Rodney Parade. It was now around four in the morning as she once again left her arse print on the green, green grass of home. On this occasion it felt less passionate and a bit more like hard work. Halfway through I felt relieved that I hadn't played for Swansea, Neath and Llanelli as well! I did consider taking her to Crumlin to finish off my own little Triple Crown. But I knew there would have been no grass on the field.

Alas, like most new relationships, we got on well until the point it turned from sweet to very sour. To be truthful I'd just got divorced and I wasn't looking for a steady relationship, just a bit of fun.

Again, my personal life seemed to be spiralling out of control. I already felt like I was up shit creek, not only without a paddle, but with a hole in the boat the size of someone's fist. Then to add to my woes, I got banned from driving. Not once, not twice, but three times.

The first occasion reminded me of a scene from the Keystone Cops meets Butch Cassidy and The Sundance Kid, or to be precise, Spikey Cassidy and the Charlie Faulkner Kid.

I wasn't sure how, but Charlie got a job, coaching the Jewish rugby team for a tournament in the Maccabiah Games in Israel. I know what you're probably thinking, and to be honest, I thought it was a joke too. But it was all true. To get some funds, Charlie asked me if I would come along to a dinner they were hosting in London, near Kings Cross, to do a bit of a turn.

Of course I told him I would, so long as I didn't have to wear one of those hats and at the end of the night, get circumcised. I also insisted he sorted out a hotel for us for the night.

'Yes, yes the hotel will all be sorted,' he promised me.

We drove up in my Mitsubishi Galant and it turned out to be a good night. I did my little routine which went down quite well. After a few beers and a couple of wines, Charlie dropped the bombshell. 'Sorry Spike, but they.......forgot to book us any rooms.'

I knew I shouldn't, but I decided to drive home. It was two in the morning, with hardly any other traffic on the M4. I stayed well within the speed limits. Then halfway home, Charlie piped up, 'I'm starving.'

'Lets keep going Charl...we're not far from home.'

'But I'm starving. Let's stop for a piss break and a bacon sandwich.'

I didn't want to, but I agreed, so I pulled into Leigh Delamere services.

He couldn't get a normal bacon sandwich as they'd sold out. Instead he had to buy some scabby old bacon, then the bread and butter separately. The self-made sandwich ended up costing him a fortune.

When we came out, I clocked some coppers sitting in a car, drinking coffee, in the corner of the services. Acting as normally as possible, I drove away. I'd only been on the road for about five minutes or less, when their Range Rover appeared behind me with its blue and red lights flashing.

'Bloody hell, the police,' I muttered.

It was then Charlie came out with the first of his immortal lines of the night, 'Hit the gas, Spike.' A dollop of brown sauce fell off his chin onto his shirt.

Stupidly, I did what Charlie told me. My car was a mean machine. We left the cops for dead. Then Charlie came up with an even better line which I will take to my grave. As we saw the Severn Bridge in the distance, he yelled, 'Quick Spikey, let's high tail it over the border.'

'Charlie, where the hell, do you think we are going...?Mexico? You daft bastard.'

But I was the daft one. I was the one who thought I could actually outrun the law. I put my foot right down and headed for God's Own Country. Of course, another police car sat waiting on the bridge, with a big grin all over its bonnet.

To be fair, the coppers weren't too bad, even though Charlie kept butting in.

'Have you had a drink, sir,' I was asked.

'No,' Charlie chipped in, 'we've been talking to the Jews in London like. We've been to a very important do.' The copper thought he was taking the piss. I blew into the bag. It came out just over the limit. One of the cops drove us back to Chippenham police station. Because I was only just over, we were in the station for less than an hour, had a few mugs of tea and they let us go.

I got a one year ban and a big fine but it could of been worse. Thinking about it they could have done me for a variety of other offences like speeding, making a run for it, and harbouring a known bloody idiot!

I could have strangled Charlie.

The second driving ban came about a year later. I'd just finished a heavy gym session in the Sun health club in Newport with my training partner, a big strong power lifter called Irish George.

I had started to get my act together and trained with him every Saturday. Then we would go across to the Rising Sun pub for a few beers. This day, I had a few drinks, but nothing excessive because I had a BBQ that evening in my village.

While I was having a laugh with the boys, an ex-girlfriend appeared like a ghost from the past. She had turned into a bit of a bunny boiler since breaking up. I couldn't go anywhere without her popping up.

She wanted me to go with her for a drive. I told her no. She made a big scene and stormed out, to the amusement of all the old timers in the bar. At five o clock, I jumped in my car. I hadn't gone two hundred metres when a cop car screeched up in front of me, and another one blocked me in from behind.

'Just a routine check,' the copper said.

'Routine check, yeah I bet.'

Again, I got done for being just over. I asked the arresting office why they had stopped me. I could tell they had been tipped off and were waiting for me. He wouldn't say, but did let slip that they had a phone call from a female to say I was drinking. There's nothing like the revenge of a woman scorned, or so I've been told.

I got banned for three years.

The third time, a few years later, I'm sure it was just plain old police harassment. I had a black Mercedes with my own number plate. I had a job as a rep for a chemical company. I was also doing some coaching at that time.

I was unsure who I had upset. Maybe Inspector Crawford, the ref at Bristol, had a contract taken out on me! At that time I was getting stopped by the old Bill at least once a month. In the end I just got used to it. 'Routine checks', I was always told.

One Tuesday night, Rumney, the team I coached, had just won the league with eight games still left to play. Again, not learning my lesson I sank a few beers to celebrate. To cut a long story short, I got done again. This time, I expected to go over the wall, and get a prison sentence.

I had to go and see a group of probation officers before the court hearing to explain why I shouldn't be locked up. Basically, I was begging for my freedom. A team of people were waiting to interview me and for various reasons I was not in the best state of mind. It was another real low point in my life.

'Why shouldn't we give you a custodial sentence?' one of them glared at me.

'Look,' I said, 'if you think you want to send me to prison, just do it. If you think it's a good thing, I can't stop you. But I do coach a rugby team, I do coach mini and juniors, so if I go down, their coach will be gone.' I added, 'I have been caught before but in all other cases very marginally. I will lose my job, and become another statistic on the dole. But it's up to you.

Do what you feel fit!' I meant every word of it, and gave the performance of my life.

In the end, they decided not to send me to prison. They gave me another long driving ban.

I was relieved, but I still had the difficult task of trying to make a living as a salesman without being able to drive my company car. A year or two earlier, I'd got a job as a salesman for a Cardiff-based chemical corporation whose owner had personally head-hunted me for the role. I started off on less than ten grand a year, but with a promise of a directorship if everything went well. I quickly became Welsh Sales Manager. I had good contacts and people seemed to like me. Soon I was earning over £3k a month.

So getting banned for the third time didn't help my work situation, but instead of moaning about it, I used my loaf and got someone to drive me to my appointments. At times I even hopped on the bus to go and see my customers. They could see my dedication and my sales actually improved.

However, although I was outselling the other salesmen, the company owner saw my driving ban as a convenient way to get rid of me and I got the sack.

I took the case went to an industrial tribunal; my main gripe being that my contract never said that I had to have a car. As long as my figures were ok, that should have been enough. I also proved I had the best sales figures, with or without me driving. The owner knew that I had been banned for a year in 1990, but never warned me that I would lose my job if I got disqualified again.

Because of who I was, and had been in my rugby life, it again became quite a high profile case in Wales. The newspapers reported the hearing each day. In the end the tribunal in Cardiff ruled it was unfair dismissal, but added that my behaviour had contributed to the sacking.

Due to this, my compensation payout was cut in half and the settlement was peanuts, considering what I had been earning.

I began to wonder if my life could get any lower. I hadn't worked for about six months; I lived in a rented place with little money coming in, and was getting a bit desperate. Then, out of the blue came a phone call from Terry Holmes. I hadn't seen, or spoken to, Terry for two years or more. He asked if I fancied a beer and a chat about something.

'Of course', I said, 'yes.'

Terry asked if I would like to work on a commission-only basis for an industrial supplies and chemical company he was a partner in. I told Terry I didn't have a driving licence. He said he knew. 'I read the papers Spikey.' he said. 'You used to be on the back page when you played rugby, now you are on the front pages these days Spikey, for one thing or another.'

We had a good laugh about it all.

Terry is an exceptionally private person, and one of the best family men I have known. As usual he turned out to be a true friend. He gave me the opportunity to sort my life out once again until the next time! He helped me find a new place in Bassaleg, just outside Newport. It was perfect, two bedrooms two bathrooms, but needed decorating. I thought that if my daughters ever spoke to me again and came to stay, there would at least be a bedroom for them.

Like many times before, I was on a mission. I kept hearing stories that I had lost it, but by then I don't think I had 'it' to lose in the first place. I stopped drinking and borrowed the money to do up my new apartment from top to bottom. A lot of the stuff came from very good friends who stuck by me and did not want paying until I was on my feet again. That's when you know who your true friends are. My sister Susan and some of her friends were great and helped with the decorating.

Other things for the apartment just kept falling off the back of lorries: Bathroom suites; beds; televisions and carpets. I won't say where the kitchen came from, but it was beautiful, just like they have in those top-of-the-range chalets. Visitors said they couldn't believe I lived there, it was immaculate. Saying that, I always have always been a perfectionist in everything I have ever done, once I'd set my mind on it.

# 12

# "Hello, I'm Oliver Reed"

*"Spikey's first league game as our coach was away at Llanelli. It was also Neil Jenk's first game for Ponty. We had two sent-off before halftime yet we still drew the match. In Spike's post-match interview he said 'I didn't see the two incidents but I'm happy with the draw. Now we will stay and celebrate until the sun comes up. If we had won we would be staying down here 'till next Friday!' He was made for Pontypridd. We were all so mad it worked well. We have become great friends and I have great respect for him. Mike is a proper legend of Welsh Rugby and he has been a big influence on my rugby career."*

**Nigel Bezani**
**Pontypridd**

After hitting rock bottom, as the saying goes, I had two choices. Either get my act together or end up getting washed away. I made a conscious effort to sort my life out so I gave up my spot in O'Reillys bar to some other no-hoper. I even gave up drinking, between a Monday afternoon and a Tuesday morning...ha ha. No, I really did go on the wagon for a while.

Mentally, I got to a much better place. I still had days when the blues kicked in hard, but the lows weren't as painful as they had been.

When I first retired I was asked by a number of local clubs if I fancied coaching. At that time, it was the last thing I wanted to do. I needed a complete break from the sport and the arseholes running it. Then after a few years I mellowed a little, and I thought 'why not, maybe it would be like therapy.' *'Hello, my name's Spikey Watkins, I used to be a practicing rugby lunatic'*

Pontypridd were looking for a coach and they thought I would fit the bill. Ponty, around that time, were an unfashionable, rough-and-tumble Valley outfit with lots of promise but nothing much to show for all their efforts. The season before I went there, they finished second from bottom of the league table, one place above the pond life on the coast.

My brief from the Committee was plain and simple, 'Just keep us up'.

Since I had been out of the game, the world and its dog had turned professional. A lot of foreign coaches arrived to 'teach' us how to play our national sport. These guys came here with big egos and high wages to tell us the bleeding obvious. Get fit, stop drinking 12 pints of beer after each match and get more professional off the field as well as on it. That's not rocket science, is it?

Charlie had parted ways with the Jewish team by then and got involved with my old side, Cardiff. The Australian coach Alex Evans had brought a lot of new ideas and methods to the capital city club. Alex, who later went on to coach Wales in a World Cup campaign, was regarded as a guru of the game.

When Charlie found out I was about to coach Ponty, he was on the blower straight away. 'Look now Spike, rugby's changed since our day. There's brand new training methods now, see. We'll have to meet up and I can run you through some of the drills.'

I couldn't wait. We met up in Tredegar Park, just off the M4 near Newport. He arrived in his car with a bag of balls and two contact tackle pads. 'Right Spikey, I'll go through a few little drills to help you.'

He handed me one of the pads. I could see the confusion on his face. 'I need someone else,' he muttered.

'But Charl, there's only me and you. Use a tree.'

'I can't use a bloody tree.'

Just then a guy in his late forties appeared over the mound walking a small dog. Charlie shouted over, 'Oh butt, give us a hand for five minutes.'

'What?'

'Can you hold this pad for a few minutes?'

'I'm walking my dog, mate.'

Charlie tutted, 'Well tie him to the tree over there.'

'I told you we would end up using a tree,' I piped up.

After some persuasion the guy tied the dog up and like a fish out of water held on tightly to the other pad. Charlie gave us instructions. I stood with a tackle pad about ten yards away from him and the other guy stood about ten yards further back than me.

Charlie shouted ready, and with ball in hand, he barged into me, pretending to offload the ball. 'See Spike, before contact, you must offload ball. It's all about offloading the ball.'

'Oh that's good Charl.' I thought, 'bloody hell, we got someone to come all the way from Oz to show us that.'

Nonetheless Charlie got fully lost in the moment. He continued running at the man, who must have weighed about 11 stone soaking wet. The guy's face froze as the 18 stone Welsh rhino charged towards him. Charlie's shoulder not only connected with the pad but bowled the poor guy over as well. The man lay on the grass, flat on his back. Charlie looked down at him and said, 'Hey butt, if you're going to do this properly, show a bit of commitment.'

In shock, the man clambered to his feet and hobbled away. I'm still not sure who learnt the biggest lesson that day, me or the guy with the dog?

With Charlie's words of wisdom ringing in my ears, I set about on my first ever coaching adventure. And what a great adventure it turned out to be. It turned out to be one of the best times of my life. The players at Ponty were a dream to work with, a great set of boys, who didn't give a toss about anyone. My kind of players. They had no super stars playing for them at the time, although many of them went on to represent Wales, at various levels, and in Neil Jenkins's case, the British Lions.

When I first went there, Jenks was just an 18 year-old kid. But what dedication he had. He would always be out on the field practicing his kicking. After training finished, he'd still be out there until 11 o clock some nights. On odd occasions I had to drag him off the pitch. He would still be begging me to let him have one more kick. Once, I turned the floodlights off or we'd never have got him out of there.

I knew I had to make a good impression at my first training session with the Ponty guys. In my playing days I hadn't completely won the hearts and minds of their fans and the players. In one of my last mid-week games for Newport, against Ponty at a packed house in Sardis Road, someone went down injured. While waiting for the lineout, I began to entertain the crowd by throwing the ball up in the air and catching it behind my back. Phil John, a tough little hooker who should have gone on to play for Wales, strolled up and called me a big headed bastard. As he walked away, I bounced the ball off the top of his head. Steam shot out of his ears, like a cappuccino machine. He wanted to kill me and so did the fans.

So I knew I had a lot of making up to do.

In my first session, I sat all the players, the likes of Steele

Lewis, Nigel Bezani, Jonathan Mason and of course, Phil, down on the grass. Phil just sat there growling at me. Another new face was Dale McIntosh, now known throughout the world as The Chief. He'd come over from New Zealand to play in Wales. A mountain of a man, who looked at me as if he could bite my head off in one chomp. I looked at him and thought,' he's my way in'. In front of everyone I pointed at The Chief and said. 'Hey, do you know we are related son.'

He looked at me and shook his head, 'Nah, we ain't.'

'We are, we are related.'

'Nah. I'm from New Zealand...we can't be.'

'We are...we go back a long way.'

'How do you work that out?' I could see him tensing up, a frown on his face.

'Well your great, great grandfather ate my great, great grandfather.'

Everyone burst out laughing. Luckily, the Chief did the same. The ice was broken and now we could get down to the serious stuff. By the end of that session, I think the entire team would have run through a brick wall for me.

What I liked most was that each player worked for one another and looked out for each other. They were really good mates off the field as well as on. They carried no airs or graces and had no prima donnas. I wanted a wild bunch, but a wild bunch that could play a bit as well and that's just what I got.

I actually picked Neil Jenkins for his first senior game ever. A nice, easy trip down to Llanelli to face the Welsh league champions, in our first competitive game of the season.

Our game plan was simple; don't get beaten by a cricket score. That got thrown out of the window within three minutes, when our flanker Denzil Earland got sent off for stamping. I feared the worst, especially when our man-monster of a second row, Big Jim Scarlet, who not only looked like he lived on a caravan site but actually did, received his marching orders at the start of the second half.

Everyone thought we were dooooomed! But with me on the side lines jumping up and down like a mad-man and what was left of my team performing like Spikey's Heroes we didn't do half bad. In fact, Llanelli only salvaged a draw with a last minute try.

After the match, Gerald Davies interviewed me for TV. 'There were a few unsavoury incidents, Spikey, do you think your players were a bit too robust?'

'Not at all, Gerald,' I grinned at him, 'I think we were hard done by and got robbed in the end. My boys played with a pride and a passion that's been lacking in Welsh rugby for many a year. I'm proud of every one of them.'

I went into our changing rooms, slammed the door and said, 'You bunch of stupid bastards, we could have won that game....but I love you all. That was bloody brilliant.'

That was the start of a great roller-coaster ride for us that season. I had to hold the boys back. They were mad for it. If I'd told them to rob a bank they would have done it for me.

We went down to Neath and their coach Brian Thomas called us the Pontypridd Upstarts. Then everyone started to take notice. Within no time we were feared by all the big clubs.

Like I said, my goal had been to keep them in the division. However, I nearly ended up killing a few of them after one training session. We'd had a few beers in the club one Wednesday night when someone suggested going to the Globe pub for a few more. It was only about half a mile away. I know I should have walked but I wanted to show off my new car; a green, Golf VR6. The original flying machine.

'Let's walk, Spike,' the Chief said.

'No, don't be stupid, get in.'

About five of them piled in. Dale himself was the size of a fully grown elephant, so you can imagine how tight it was. We had to fold Neil Jenkins's ears back just to be able to close the car doors.

I took off like a rocket and, looking back, I was driving like an idiot. All the boys sat in the car, screaming. Next thing, I struggled to take the corner. The car hit the kerb. The steering column snapped off in my hand. I lost control. The car flew through the air, rolled over several times before landing on its roof in the middle of the road.

It was like going back in time with Pipper Watkins on the M4.

Everything in the car went silent. I looked across at the Chief. His face was ghost white. I thought, 'oh no, I've killed him. I am definitely going to prison for the rest of my life now.'

'You bloody idiot,' the Chief boomed, 'you could have bloody killed us.'

I smiled, more in relief than anything else. We all clambered out. The car lay in the middle of the road on its roof, a write-off. My old man had warned me that green was an unlucky colour. Maybe he was right.

'Let's get it the right way up and then go for a pint' I said. 'I don't want to spoil a good evening.' They all looked at me as if I was mental. 'It's too late crying over spilt milk.' We turned the car back the right way up and went for a beer.

I wasn't the only mental one in the club. One time we played a cup game against Pyle. The lower league club had a promotion on Tennant's Extra and, unwisely, put two free kegs on for us after the match.

Everyone got tanked up and Steele (Stella) Lewis started arm wrestling against the Chief. They were always having a go at each other. At almost every training session someone had to pull them apart.

'Don't now boys,' I warned them, 'it will end in tears.'

They didn't listen. Everyone in the hall crowded over them to watch. Neither of them would give in. Stella began to get the better of the contest. I could tell by the grimace on his face, the Chief was struggling. Suddenly, he locked his jaws onto Stella's thumb and bit down. Stella screamed before whacking Dale full force on the jaw, knocking him off the chair. Then all hell broke loose. Tables and chairs went over, glasses smashed. The both of them rolled about on the floor like mad men, punching seven bells out of each other. Ponty players tried to pull them apart. The Pyle players and committee didn't know what the hell was going on.

We eventually separated them. Then the tears flowed. They sat in the corner hugging and cwtching and telling each other how much they loved one another for the rest of the night.

'Boys,' I called the other players around them, 'that's what we are about.'

Using my motivational skills I think I helped inspire the passion bubbling away under the surface in Ponty. I got the best out of the players, and I think the players got the best out of me. We had one hell of a year, both off and on the field.

Although we finished third that season I decided to leave the club. It had nothing to do with Ponty. I still had problems in my personal life and I found it really hard to mix the two.

However, I'd like to believe I helped to build a team with a reputation and an attitude which stayed with the Valley club until the powers-to-be destroyed it all when they introduced regional rugby and left Ponty and the rest of the Valleys with nothing. Probably the biggest ever injustice in Welsh sport.

I'm quite proud of how I helped many of the players from that so-called unfashionable club to get into the Welsh set up. When Neil got into the Welsh squad, I got interviewed to tell the Welsh public what he was like. I said he was more of a southern hemisphere type of number 10 than the traditional jinking Welsh outside halves of the 70's. I said he was a Grant Fox type of player, a great distributor of the ball as well as being a fantastic goal kicker and he went on to prove me right.

Along with the rest of the Ponty boys, he was a diamond. And if I must step out of character to say a few words, so were the Pontypridd committee. They were a real pleasure to do business with.

I did coach again when everything settled down in my hectic life. Like I mentioned, I took the reins at Rumney in Cardiff for a very successful 5 years. During that time, we got promoted from Division 5 to Division 1. Then I coached closer to home when, for a number of seasons, I was in charge at Newbridge with Jonathan Westwood.

My last appointment saw me as team manager of Cross Keys. They had been struggling and finished bottom of the Championship table. It was hard work, but enjoyable. Often the most difficult things to achieve prove to be the most satisfying. I helped to create a buzz there and they ended up doing quite well.

Away from the coaching I had some bizarre but memorable experiences. One Sunday afternoon I was at home in the garden, cutting the grass when I got a phone call from the owner of the village pub.

'Hey, Spikey, you need to come down, there's some people here who want to meet you.'

'I haven't got time.'

'You have to come down. There's someone special here asking about you, quick, hurry up'

'Who is it?'

He wouldn't tell me over the phone. I thought a pint sounded better than cutting the rest of the grass anyway. So wearing a pair of tracksuit bottoms and an old tee-shirt I walked into the

Castle pub, where I had the shock of my life. There, sitting in the corner, larger than life, was none other than, Oliver Reed. Apparently he loved his rugby and was down visiting an old friend in Crumlin. My name had popped up in conversation, the good bits and the bad, and Ollie had demanded to meet me.

'Hello Spikey,' he shook my hand, 'I'm Oliver Reed.'

'Hello Oliver Reed, I'm Spikey.'

What an afternoon we had. Drinking, swapping stories, more drinking, more stories, more drinking. I laughed non-stop. We both did. He told me incredible tales of Burton, Richard Harris and himself, the original British Brat Pack. I told stories about the wonderful world of Charlie. I think he thought I was making them up!

Later that evening, he tried to get me to go on a pub crawl with him, but I had to get home. Apparently, worse for wear, he staggered back to the Maes Manor Hotel in Blackwood, where he was staying and ended up naked, swinging from one of the chandeliers. That's the effect I had on people. I bet he looked more frightening than that bloody Orang-utan who'd crept into my room in South Africa.

Another interesting meeting happened when I was visiting my daughter in Hull University. One afternoon we were in a pub called the Mainbrace and I got up on the stage and did a bit of a turn. Later on when I was by the bar, some scruffy guy wearing a big overcoat stood next to me. I noticed he had long nails for a man. He told me he really enjoyed my act and wanted to buy me a pint. We had a few and chatted away about this and that. He was a really nice, and extremely knowledgeable, guy. When he went to the loo, my daughter came rushing up.

'Do you know who that is?'

'Yeah, some guy, Paul.'

'Yeah...it's Paul Heaton from the Beautiful South.'

'Who? That scruffy so and so?' I thought I recognised him. I liked their music and I liked his first band, The Housemartins.

When he came back I said. 'Oh butt, I heard you are a bit of a turn yourself, aren't you?'

Modestly, he just nodded his head. We drank all afternoon. He told me stories of the band and the inspiration behind some of the songs. I told stories of the wonderful world of Charlie. Again, I think he thought I was making them up!

A gallon or so of beer later, he went back to his house, stripped naked, and swung from the light shade. That's the effect I had on people. No, he didn't do that. Well I don't think he did anyway.

Paul and I became good mates and every time I went there we would meet up for a few beers. He promised me that whenever the band played in Wales he would sort me out a few tickets. A few months later I had a message on my answering machine telling me he had left 10 tickets for me at the booking office in the CIA. The following week, I rounded a few mates up and we headed to Cardiff. As we were walking to the venue, I thought, 'this is going to be embarrassing if there are no tickets for us'. I needn't have worried. Paul was more than true to his word. Not only did we get tickets, we also got backstage passes. Better still, during the gig he shouted out, 'Hope you're out there, Spikey. We'll have a few beers after.'

It was a great show and we all ended up partying in the Marriott Hotel until the early hours. Only thing was, Paul was disappointed I hadn't taken along the wonderful Charlie.

Then a few things happened that started to drag me back into my pit of depression. First off, the photo of me playing for Wales was mysteriously nicked from the locked cabinet at Newport Rugby Club and apparently thrown into the river. Someone told me what had happened, but he didn't say who did it. I had my suspicions and still do. There had been five Captains of Newport, who had played for Wales since the war, Dai Watkins, Brian Price, two others and me. All five photos had been in the locked cabinet.

When I played for Wales, the club wanted a photo of me for the cabinet.

'Thanks,' I said, 'that's a great idea. Where do you want me to have it done?'

'It's up to you to get it done,' they informed me.

I thought they were joking. I was Captain of the Club and Captain of Wales and they wanted me to pay for my own photo to put in their bloody trophy cabinet. Take a running jump I told them. In the end, they used a photo of me from a newspaper and blew it up so large I looked like Dennis the Menace.

So, unless Plug from the Bash Street Kids had pinched my photo, I wanted to know if it was true. I also wanted to know why I had been singled out. I had retired years before. I couldn't understand why someone would do it.

I stormed down to the club to see for myself. A committeeman stopped me on the door. 'You can't come in, you are not a member,' he said.

'Not a member. I was Captain of this Club for four years. I just want to see if its true about my photo going missing.'

'You've only come here to cause trouble. This is a member's only lounge. If you don't go I will call the police.'

I said, 'Trouble! If you don't get out of the way, you will see what trouble is.' I ignored him and marched passed.

My sources had been spot on. My photo had gone. Thankfully I didn't kick off right there in the lounge. I bit my lip and went home, upset.

Even today, I put a brave face on about it and say I don't care that someone took my photo down and destroyed it. But deep down that's a lie. I did care. I played for them for a very long time. I gave them everything I had. I think I deserved a little respect.

To top it all, they sent me a solicitor's letter saying it had been brought to their attention I had abused a committeeman. They told me I was banned from entering the club and would only be allowed back in when hell freezes over. That suited me down to the ground.

But it wasn't just the Newport club which had got under my skin. I hated going to the town itself. One afternoon I went shopping in Newport market and saw a gang of yobs running through the streets. One of them knocked an old lady over. All her shopping spilled-out, all over the pavement. I went to chase after them, but they disappeared. I bent down and helped the old lady with her stuff.

I looked across the road and saw a copper standing in a doorway. 'Why didn't you do something about that, you tosser?' I yelled across at him.

'Oh, I'll do something about you if you talk to me like that,' he batted back.

I couldn't believe it. I called him a few more choice names under my breath and carried on picking up the old woman's shopping.

He spoke into his radio. Within five minutes a Black Maria turned up. Eight coppers jumped out of the back and surrounded me. They must have suspected I was a terrorist or something, come to blow up the centre of Newport. That would have caused all of £30 worth of damage.

'You are under arrest sir,' one of them said.

'No, you got the wrong person,' the old woman stuck up for me, 'this gentleman helped me.'

They wouldn't listen. They handcuffed me and led me towards the van.

'What are you doing?' I yelled, 'There's something wrong

with you.' I glared at the copper who had been standing in the doorway.

It was Saturday afternoon. I hadn't been drinking or anything. I'd been in a good mood before all this broke out. They carted me off to the police station. By the time I got there, I was incensed.

Again, the Sergeant on the desk knew me. He asked me what was going on. I told him without holding back.

'Don't worry I'll sort it out.' He came back and told me I could go.

But by then I didn't want to go. I wanted justice. 'No,' I dug my heels in, 'I'm not going anywhere. I want to know why I was arrested.'

'Don't give us a hard time now, Spike,' the Sergeant begged me. 'Just go home please.'

I wouldn't move. After they threatened to arrest me again, I said, 'Ok I'll go but since you carted me off, you can take me back to where you picked me up.'

'We haven't got any transport.'

'You transported me here when you arrested me for nothing.' I sat down.

The old lady from the precinct appeared in the cop shop. She'd made the effort to come down carrying her shopping to see how I was. 'This gentleman tried to help me,' she said to the Sergeant.

'We know, he's free to go.'

In the end they were begging me to go. I wouldn't. I sat there like a stubborn donkey. I pictured them dragging me out and throwing me into the road, like bouncers in a nightclub throwing out a trouble maker, and then locking the cop shop door.

I finally left. But I was positive the police had singled me out for 'special attention'.

When I coached Newbridge, a copper in the team warned me to be careful because he had heard some of the police were out to get me. I wasn't a criminal. I must have upset someone along the way.

That night after the incident in Newport town centre, I decided to make a new life for myself. I knew if I stayed I would end up in trouble. I'm sorry to say it, but the environment, mixed with my personality, just brought out the worst in me. On top of that there was little or no work in the Valleys. Factories were shutting down right, left and centre. There was nothing left for me.

I needed to get out, and then an opportunity came knocking from an unusual source.

# 13

# Hooker Goes to Bangkok

*"I was brought up watching Spike applying his trade in Wales. I always took an interest in his career as he was a friend of my father and a local rugby celebrity. I had the pleasure and privilege of working with Spike at Newbridge RFC, where we were joint head coaches for a fantastic five-year period. Spike was a terrific colleague; he has outstanding knowledge and is the greatest motivator I have witnessed. His honesty was brutal, but a breath of fresh air in a game with so many fraudulent individuals, and boy could he smell one of those frauds. A great man and a great friend, loyal to the end."*

**Jonathan Westwood**
**Newport - Cardiff - Neath**
**Ebbw Vale - Aberavon - Cross Keys**

Did I ever think I would up-sticks and leave Wales to go settle in a completely different country with a completely different culture? I'm not sure. I had a feeling I would end up somewhere else. I just didn't quite know where. I always enjoyed travelling around the world in my rugby days. It's strange but I often believed I was accepted and taken more seriously in other countries other than Wales.

Like Charlie 'the guru' Faulkner once told me, 'Spikey, you

will never be a prophet in your own land.' Profound, even for Charlie! Mind you he also reckoned, 'we won the Second World War because we kept our pilots in a darkened room and fed them carrot cake so their eyesight was much better than the Germans.' And he believed every word of it.

I think the circumstances surrounding me dictated what I did. If I'd had a good job in Wales, and been in a relationship that was strong and loving, I probably wouldn't have left. I was living in Bassaleg, a lovely little village, and in a beautiful condo but I had just split up from a long term relationship and was living alone.

Bouts of depression still gripped me tightly from time to time. I tried my best to shake myself free. But it was a strong, stubborn little so-and-so and on many occasions it engulfed me. I went for days without going out or speaking to anyone. I would sit on my settee dressed in my rugby kit wearing my Welsh cap, while throwing darts at cardboard cut-outs of WRU committeemen. No I didn't do that, I wasn't that sick. But thinking of it, I wished I had now!

Work-wise I was a struggling, self-employed, salesman. I got paid, or not, on a commission-only basis selling industrial chemical supplies to local industries and whoever else I could get to buy from me. Some years had been good to me, but those good times had slowly vanished! Factories I had dealt with were closed or downsized dramatically. It was as if someone had switched the lights out throughout the Valleys.

Opening new accounts became hard work with little reward. I'd find myself in an office with some smart-arsed buyer fresh out of college. They didn't want to buy from me. They just wanted to see people like me beg them for an order. I think it gave them some kind of thrill. I wouldn't do that; my dignity would never allow it.

In the end I just couldn't make a living in Wales. The way it was heading, if I had stayed, God only knows where I would have ended up. I don't even want to think about it. I needed a fresh start to prevent me going completely off my rocker. Also, I definitely didn't want to be one of those sad, old men sitting on a bar stool in some rugby club reminiscing about the try they scored in 1982. Of course, I'm proud of what I did, immensely proud. That's the primary reason for writing this book. I wanted people to know the real me and what I had gone through. But that particular chapter in my life had come to an end and it was time to turn to a fresh page and write a new adventure for myself.

A phone call from a good friend made me poke my head out of the Welsh goldfish bowl and go in search of sandy beaches, bounty bars and girls with five o'clock shadows.

For years, a really good mate of mine, Nigel Mochrie, had been asking me to go and spend some time in Thailand. During one telephone conversation he mentioned a lovely lady he knew, a school teacher whose husband had died tragically. He had been a courier bike rider for one of the major banks in Bangkok. One morning, taking letters from one bank to another, he was hit by a bus and died instantly.

'Maew, his widow,' Nigel said, 'would be perfect for you and you would be perfect for her.'

'What's the catch, Nigel?' I asked.

'There's no catch....just come over and meet her.'

I didn't believe him for one minute. In my naïve, narrow mind, every woman in Thailand either worked in titty bars, was a hooker or a good looking ladyboy waiting for the chop. Or all three!

I asked him which she was.

He didn't reply. Instead, he sent me her photo and email address. I thought, 'what have I got to lose?' so I started contacting her. What I didn't know was that at that time Maew didn't speak any English. Her daughter read all my emails to her and on her instructions, wrote all of her replies.

After a few weeks of internet romancing, I decided to go and meet her in person. What was the worst that could happen? If it didn't work out I could just hop back home on a plane or bag myself one of those ladyboys!!

I arrived at the recently opened Suvarnabhumi Airport in Bangkok. It had that new smell, like a brand new car and I stood in the arrival hall, looking around and trying to spot her. Part of me wondered if the photo I had seen of her had been a fake. I began to picture her waddling through the crowd like the not-so-good-looking fat Thai bride, Ting Tong, in the Little Britain sketch.

That image disappeared the moment I was surrounded by eight Thai women. I didn't know what the hell was going on. They smiled and bowed at me. I didn't know if they were out to fleece me or kidnap me. Maybe they thought I was famous, the rugby version of Tom Jones.

Then they pushed this beautiful lady in front of me. Maew stood there, like a frightened rabbit, her eyes staring down at the floor.

'Hello,' I said, and held out my hand.

The women giggled and shrieked with excitement. They all gave me good luck cards they had made in school and hand-in-hand, we walked out into the sunshine and the intense heat of a new life.

At the start we lived apart. She lived in Bangkok, and I stayed with Nigel down in Pattaya. We met every weekend. When I arrived by bus in the city, she would be waiting for me with a bottle of water, and a bag of pineapple! I loved that.

After a couple of months there, I decided to go back home to Wales for a while. I got my head down and stuck into work, but no matter what I did, I still couldn't earn a decent living.

What's more, it was winter, it was dark, wet and cold both inside and out!

I was fifty four and living a nightmare. There were very few places I could go out and really enjoy myself without getting into trouble. I kept up my training regime, but after that there was only the pub and I certainly didn't want to get dragged back down into that way of life again. I didn't want my spot in O'Reillys back.

In typical Welsh fashion, everywhere I went people talked about the same sad things. Who had died? Who had lost their jobs? Who'd had an operation? And who was having an affair with whom? No one talked about the future, or wanted to do something different with their lives. Everyone seemed happy just to look backwards instead of moving forwards.

I wanted more and in the end the decision to move to Thailand was a no-brainer. The cost of living was so much cheaper and the weather was so much warmer. Even though the people didn't have much, they seemed to smile a lot more and of course; there was Maew, the first woman who didn't want to change me. She was so caring and loving towards me. She became, and still is, my rock.

It took Maew a few weeks to tell me she had two children of her own, a daughter of 14 and a boy, a year younger. She was afraid, I guess, that I wouldn't accept them and maybe reject her. It must have been a difficult period in all of their lives. On top of that, I could have been a pervert or whatever. There are some strange men lurking about in these parts. She had to be careful and I fully respect her for that.

Also, at first she was embarrassed to show me her house. It was quite run down, but more importantly for me, it was very clean and tidy. Structurally it needed a lot of work done to it so I decided to help her refurbish it, in order that we could live there for a few years.

Her children accepted me from the start, which was fantastic for me. On one occasion, Maew's daughter won an award for being the number one pupil in her state school. There is private education in Thailand but it is very expensive. For her to achieve this award was a real big thing. She came home and said, 'Hey Daddy, will you come with me to get my award.'

I had a lump in my throat.

There were over 2,000 people in the auditorium early that morning. Everyone sat crossed legged on the floor. Never mind playing in big games for Wales, nothing compared to how nervous I felt as I was about to walk towards the stage with her. I gripped Fai's hand. 'I'm really nervous,' I whispered.

She squeezed my hand and replied, 'I'll look after you Daddy.'

I walked down the aisle through the crowds, as proud as punch, tears rolling down my cheeks. Everyone stared at me. I was the only European in the room. I was told later, I had been the only European to have ever done that in the school.

I sat on the stage, shaking like a leaf with Fai sat down by my feet. Apparently, their head should never be higher than their elders, which is a mark of great respect. I've done a lot of emotional things over the years with my own family but to do that was something I'll never forget.

My driving ambition at this moment in my life is to get Maew's children, Fai and Tee, through University so they get a good grounding in life. The city and the country can be unforgiving at times. They need all the help I can give them and I'm only too glad to do it! Fai is well on her way and won a six month internship with Etihad Airlines, another great achievement.

Often I would go along to Maew's school and I got to know the kids and the teachers very well. I even once had the entire school out in the yard playing rugby. I bought all the teachers

Welsh rugby T-shirts. They put them on and taught the kids in them all day and have worn them over and over again.

I think my daughters back in Wales were happy for me to leave because they wouldn't have to listen to some bullshit story about their father, true or otherwise. Now they only have to listen to some bullshit story about me in Thailand.

They are now women with families of their own. They have their own lives to live, and I guess they don't want an interfering father hanging around. They know where I am. We Skype a lot and my daughters and their husbands have been over here on holidays. They know Maew very well and understand the relationship I have with her, so they are cool about everything.

My mates back home didn't really know what to think when I said I was going to Thailand to live. They knew that if I said I was going to do something, I was going to do it. Many said I was crazy, but they knew that anyway!!!

Mind you, when I first went there, I bet most thought I wouldn't survive. 'Spikey....Thailand ...Thai lady .....Big problem!!!! They assumed I would get washed down the pan in the big, bad, wolf which is Bangkok. But I'm far too sharp for that! I actually survived quite well.

Living here has, I feel, made me a lot more tolerant person. All the karma floating about and the Buddhist way of life has given me a different perspective on everything. Bangkok is one crazy city but when you are not a tourist and actually live there, it's good. I don't go walking around covered in beads with a shaven head, or anything. Well not yet!

The one regret I do have is that perhaps I should have come to Thailand sooner, but fate is fate. As my mother would say via her clairvoyants, 'what is meant to be is meant to be'. I am sure she is looking down and guiding me. In Thailand the culture is all about living a calm and peaceful life. They believe you get back what you put in. Perhaps I was born in the wrong place. I think if you grow up in an aggressive environment, it makes you aggressive. I know I can be quite volatile, quite spikey on occasions. But out in Thailand I feel more chilled out and I don't have the same problems.

When I first settled down there, I knew no one except Nigel, but I soon made many friends. I was at a function where Jonathan Davies, the great Welsh outside half, was speaking in Bangkok. He recognised me and started telling the audience some story about our experiences together. He gave me a good mention, fair play. After the event, lots of people came over to introduce themselves. Me and Gareth Hughes, the Managing Director of the RSM Thailand Accountant and Legal Firm got on like a house on fire. I soon started doing consulting work for him and got involved with the British Chamber of Commerce and the British Embassy. I spoke at Rotary dinners and Round Table events all over the South East Asian region, not just Thailand.

I'm probably most proud of the charity work I have been involved in for the Catholic Church in Bangkok, raising over £10,000 in a single year for Father Joe Maier and Sister Joan. I get lots of pleasure from helping organise and chairing many of their fundraising charity auction events. My good friend, Les Miles has done a wonderful job in getting people back in the UK to donate personal items for the cause such as boxing gloves from Joe Calzaghe, a suit from Roger Jenkins the power boat champion and lots and lots of items from famous sportsmen like Fergus Slattery, Steve Fenwick, Gareth Bale and Shane Williams. Without Les we wouldn't have raised half as much.

Of course there is a darker side to life in Bangkok, as we all know. But even those sinister edges have embraced me. I seem, to say the least, to be a more sociable person out here although I still attract wild and wonderful characters like bees around a honey pot. I can be a cheeky so-and-so at times, and not shy in coming forward. I started frequenting a well-known Irish bar called Molly Malone's, a place packed with every sort of individual you can imagine, from out-and-out bullshitters, to criminals, to successful businessmen, to people who are genuinely looking for a change of life style. I like to take people at face value. I never judge anyone until I get to know them for myself.

Luckily, it was in Molly's I witnessed something in my early days in Bangkok which made me realise I really was in a different country with a different culture set, which I needed to respect, or else!

There was an Irish musician entertaining the mainly ex-pat crowd in the bar. During his set he started making derogatory comments about Thai people, especially the women. During the break an undercover police general, who looked more like a model than a copper, quietly asked the singer to go outside for a chat.

Not thinking anything was wrong, the singer followed him outside. Allegedly, the police general led him to his armoured car and his bodyguards bungled the singer into the back. The police general pulled a gun out and calmly said, 'If you ever say anything bad about Thai people again, I will personally shoot you. And if I see you in Bangkok again, I will throw you in jail.'

The singer staggered back into the pub, as white as a ghost. He packed his stuff up and left. We never saw him again.

I learnt a big lesson that afternoon. 'You don't mess about in Thailand. You respect their culture and their people, and more importantly you make good friends with police generals!!'

And that's what I did. I got to know the people I needed to know and I didn't act like Jack the Lad. I've seen British men in bars thinking they are the bee's knees. Often they get taken to the cleaners. These Thai girls may not be educated in maths and history, but they have degrees in being streetwise. They turn these men into mincemeat with a blink of an eyelash. Believe it or not, prostitution is illegal in Thailand, but so are fake designer clothes, bags, pirate DVDs and CDs and you still see them hanging about everywhere.

I've actually heard girls telling punters, their family's only buffalo had died and there was no money to buy a new one. Or that family has had a great idea to open a fish farm back in the village, but need a little investment. Punters hand over stacks of dosh. More often than not, there are no fish farms or buffalo. Sometimes not even a family.

It's easy for these guys to get tangled up in the spider's web. These women are clever, beautiful, and very smart. They need to be. It's a tough world. Lots of these girls have nothing and come from poor families. They do it to survive. Also in Thai culture 'kindness' is seen as a weakness. So when these guys are thinking they will be liked because they are being kind, often it's not that way at all.

I was one of the lucky ones. I met Maew.

Will I ever go back home to live? Well you can never tell in life but I hope not. I've made a big life for myself out here. I love going home and seeing the boys, and watching some games at the Millennium Stadium. I miss the place, the memories, the humour, but it's a prickly place as far as I'm concerned. Bangkok is my home now. Thailand is corrupt, but it's a great place to live.

People come here for holidays, but not many jump on a plane and set up a new life here. I'm quite glad and proud I took that leap.

There is a saying that you either control Bangkok or Bangkok will control you. That's so true. No one knows what the future holds. But I do believe in the Thai philosophy and also in karma.

I am in a much better place mentally. I have a great circle of friends. One of them, Trevor Allen, once said, 'We don't have family over here in Thailand, so all our close friends are family, we look out for each other.'

He was so, so right. When our house got flooded and was four feet underwater, Trevor came to our rescue. He let us stay in his home for five weeks at no cost. That's friendship. So everything you have heard is right, you will always get a happy ending in Thailand!

I still come back to Wales at least once a year. The first time I took Maew back, we went straight to my mother and father's grave. They are buried together in Abercarn cemetery on the side of the mountain. I brought some orchids back with me to put on their grave.

I looked down and childishly said, 'Its ok Dad, you can stop spinning your head around down there, Maew is Thai, not Burmese.' I laughed to myself, but I bet he was looking up and thinking I had brought her just to annoy him. I got the impression that he thought most of the things I had done in my life, I did purely to annoy him.

So, after spilling my heart out into this book, what else is there to write? It has been one hell of a roller-coaster ride that I wouldn't recommend to anyone. From all of the extreme highs to the severe lows I have been through. I have achieved many things and messed-up many things Big Time as well. I have probably been more sinner than saint, but who's counting! And I have pissed lots of people off, some who I shouldn't have, but many who thoroughly deserved it. On saying all that, the one thing I am, is brutally honest and incredibly critical of myself, as well as others. I don't suffer fools and never will.

Whatever I've done in my life, I've given it my best shot. I know at times I've taken it right to the edge and then carried on regardless when maybe I shouldn't have, but that just the way I've been made. Some people understood me, others didn't want to.

When I was playing for Newport, a committee man, an ex-international, said to me, 'Spikey, if only you had behaved yourself, you could've been one of the all-time greats.'

My reply was, 'Hang on, I Captained Wales every time I played for them. I played in a few World XV s and captained Newport four years running. I played for the South African and UK Barbarians, plus many times for Crawshays. I had letters about my availability to go on three separate Lions tours, that's not too bad, is it?'

He looked at me and shook his head, 'See,' he replied, 'that's the trouble with you; no one can talk to you!'

I just walked away from him. That's the type of attitude I've faced all of my life. I never gave up on anything, including rugby and I was always looking to challenge myself. So once I played for Wales, let alone captaining them, I put a flag on top of that particular mountain and it was then time to find myself another mountain to climb. A bit philosophical I know, but maybe I've spent too much time with Guru Charlie! So that was my life in black and white, the good, the bad and the ugly and I hope you enjoyed it.

I will leave you with a quote written by the great Gerald Davies after I retired from the Captaincy of my country. He said, 'As captain, personality and one-man cabaret star, Mike Watkins was exactly the tonic an increasingly introverted Welsh team needed. His much needed twinkle and colour among the grey impersonality will be missed.'

# 14

# Rugby Reflections

When people found out through the grapevine that I was writing this book, I was overwhelmed by the emails and telephone calls I received offering me support and encouragement. It was fantastic. I even had a message from Alan Phillips wishing me all the best and could he come to the book launch! I told him, only if I could bring the "Hatchet" with me for old time's sake, only messing!

I also had lots of questions from individuals asking about this and that. Some of their points I dealt with in the main text, some I didn't. So I decided to try to answer the rest of the questions as honestly as I could:

1. **What was the Best Team in which you played and why?**

   The Crawshays, because when the WRU wouldn't pick me in any way, shape, or form, the likes of Arthur Rees, Neville Walsh, and Russell Jenkins of the Crawshays supported and believed in me and my rugby ability. They selected me when everyone else in Wales turned their back on me. Crawshays stuck two fingers up to the WRU and what I loved about them was that the entire set-up was run by human beings, not by small-minded dictators, wearing cheap blazers and white socks. They had a big committee, full of University-educated types, but they didn't have a committee mentality. They understood me, which I really respected them for. Also, the Crawshays motto and the focus, both on and off the field, was based on having fun, but there was always a must-win policy.

2. **What was the Best Team you played against and why?**

That must go to the Australian team during their Grand Slam tour of 1984. To me, they simply took the game to another level. They had so many world class players and they seemed to take the best parts of Rugby Union and Rugby League and fused them together to become so unbeatable. They laid down the platform for professionalism.

The Australians were also much better prepared than us and much better organised in every aspect of the game. They had been on tour for quite a few weeks before they played us and it showed. The squad had been together for a while and a lot of their players, like the Ella brothers, had come through a very successful school team. What I liked about them was they weren't afraid to be innovative or scared to take some of the Rugby League patterns of play and successfully adopt them into Union. On the other hand, in the UK and in Wales at the time, Rugby League was taboo, which was daft, because a lot of the stuff they were doing would have been perfect in Rugby Union. These days, a lot of the Rugby League concepts have been taken on board, especially in defence.

**3. If you could be remembered for just one match, what match would it be?**

The game that stands out for me was when I captained Wales to a victory against England at Twickenham in 1984. It was a massive result for us and for the whole Welsh nation (and probably all the other Celtic nations as well). We simply blew them away and the score didn't really reflect how much we were in control on that occasion. I dedicated the game to every one of the South Wales Miners who were on strike, and beating the English that day, in their own backyard, hopefully cheered them up a little during their difficult times. Plus, Terry Holmes had come back from injury to play in that match, although it was his last. I still am a big mate with Terry, so it was great to taste success with him alongside me that day.

**4. What was your favourite ground to play at?**

Without question, Cardiff Arms Park, the true home of rugby, and such a passionate crowd, win or lose. Also that night I had a jump on the half-way line probably beats any try I ever scored there!

**5. What ground did you least enjoy playing at?**

Probably Maesteg on a wet Wednesday night, after a hard day's work. It was blood, guts, thunder and broken teeth. Also Gloucester, where the entire crowd made sheep noises. I would be there throwing mud at the bastards.

214

**6. Who is the greatest player you ever played with or against?**

Danny Gerber, the South African centre, followed very, very closely by the great Terence David Holmes.

**7. Who was the Toughest Guy you ever faced?**

That's easy, my very own demons. I faced up to everyone else and either won, or had a bloody good go. My own demons proved a lot tougher to beat. I could do myself more damage than anyone else could ever do!

**8. What was your biggest disappointment as a rugby player?**

Being out of favour and snubbed by the establishment for years and years and missing out on three possible Lions tours. My rugby career nearly rocketed to the moon and beyond when I received a letter asking if I would be available, if selected, to tour, with the British Lions to New Zealand in 1977. It was hard to believe. Sadly, I never made the final cut. I received two similar letters later on in my career. One for the 1983 tour to New Zealand, but I was banned at the time and not eligible. Then again in 1986 to South Africa, but the tour was eventually cancelled due to the sporting boycott against apartheid.

**9. What was your greatest Accomplishment as Rugby Player?**

Selected to be captain of Wales on my debut, after all the trials and tribulations with WRU

**10. If you could change one rule about rugby, what would it be?**

I would bring in a rule which sanctioned the kicking in the head of props who collapse scrums on purpose! It is dangerous to collapse scrums, and, what's more, it is killing the game.

**11. Did you have any Superstitions before going out on the pitch?**

No, but when the game started I always made sure I booted my opposite number in the head within five minutes of the start.

**12. You were the first player I recall who wore his shirt collar tucked inside his shirt. It was iconic and unique. Why did you do this? And do you like the new style shirts?**

I never thought anything about the way I wore my rugby shirt. I just didn't see the need for a collar on a shirt. It wasn't as if I was ever going to wear a tie with it. So I tucked the collar inside.

It goes all the way back to my Cwmcarn Youth and Crumlin days; I just did it all my rugby days thereafter. I'm pleased to say, to the annoyance of a lot of committee men in Cardiff and Newport, who thought I was showing a lack of respect for their Club jersey, I would roll my sleeves up, or cut them off, to annoy them even more! How can you get on with the job in hand i.e. a game of rugby if you are not comfortable? I wasn't in a 'best kitted out rugby player' contest.

The sleeves were much too long on the old type jerseys anyway. 'One size fits all' was the motto. You had to have arms like a gibbon, or if you didn't before it got wet, you did after. I can still see poor little wingers, on a cold wet day, stood on the wing with the arms of their jersey dragging along the ground, in a perfect imitation of a gibbon.

I think the new type shirts are better and fit for purpose, except for scrummaging, where they are difficult to bind on to. Maybe that accounts for all the collapsed scrums in the modern game, unless the props are blaming something other than themselves.

I was in the Under Armour box in Cardiff Millennium Stadium recently. They are the kit sponsors for the Wales rugby team and I was talking to the man who is their rugby shirt designer. He told me that the new shirts are designed so it is difficult to get hold of them and need to be a very tight fit! That is no good however if you are a big fat bastard.

Mind you, if you are a poor player, you are a poor player, no matter what you are wearing. Good, or great players, could wear anything and still be great.

13. **You played against Australia and NZ and turned abroad. Were these teams more professional at that time? Did you try and get changes in the Welsh game?**

The game was already professional in my view. With 50,000 people watching games live and paying good money to go into the games. Everyone else was earning a good professional living out of the game. From the television broadcasters, the camera men, commentators, reporters, to the caterers who sold the food, to people who cut the grass and the bus, train or taxi driver who drove you to the game. The only ones who didn't get paid were the players, and the ref. When you look back it was crazy when you consider the money that was generated. Where did it go? The players weren't getting any. I never expected to make money, but nor did I expect to lose money for playing at the highest level.

Did I try to change it? Of course I did. I was always voicing an opinion to the powers-that-be. That is why I was seen as a rebel and not picked for many years. Only the people who run the Welsh Rugby Union would know the answer to that. Things had to change. Whether it was for the better is a matter of opinion.

In my opinion, we were treated like very badly but I was so proud to represent Wales and I would have put up with almost anything to play for Wales yet there is only so much you can put up with.

Things are the other way round now. Today, the players get paid a lot of money for what they are doing, and good luck to them.

**14. How do you see the demise of Welsh clubs and the birth of regions?**

For what it's worth, I don't believe the regions have worked at all. Are they even really regions? The closest to the ideal are the Ospreys, which combined Swansea and Neath, but they have underachieved with all the money they have spent down the years. Does Cardiff really represent Pontypridd and the rest of the Valleys? I don't think so! It is still Cardiff.

David Moffet must have looked at the map and thought Pontypridd was only 10 miles outside Cardiff, so it must be just a suburb of the capital. Rubbish! Pontypridd might as well be 10,000 miles away from Cardiff, as to the way people think from both places. Ten miles might be a suburb in Australia, but people are extremely proud as to where they come from here and are very deep-rooted as to who they choose to support! No-one will ever be told who to support and I love that about Wales. It makes us what we are. We are a very sensitive, proud race of people. David Moffet was allowed to put regions together only with the blessing of the WRU and the money men running the four big clubs, not the smaller but equally important ones. That's why it's all gone wrong. It should never have been allowed. Nearly all the people who allowed him to do it are still there, may I add. He must have looked at the M4 and thought 'that's handy, all these big clubs are easy to get to from the motorway.'

But Newport are still Newport, just with the Gwent Dragons bit tagged on the end to pacify the people of Gwent. They still play at Rodney Parade. They are just off the motorway as you come over the Severn Bridge; very handy for the English sides to get too. Cardiff is just down the road, and is still Cardiff. They are far removed from the Valleys. The Ospreys are 30 miles away. And of course, good old Llanelli are just down the end of the motorway. Nothing has changed. Llanelli are still Llanelli, except they play in a beautiful new stadium with hardly any people in it.

## 15. Why do you think Welsh coaches are not getting to the top? Why do we need gurus from NZ and Australia?

The problem with coaching in today's game in Wales is that everyone does the same, or appears to do the same, and it's done by the book. There is no innovation. There must be good coaches out there, but if these coaches don't conform to what the WRU stipulates, they won't get on. So they toe the line and become controlled. So they are not good coaches really, are they? They should be their own men, or women. If you are a coach, you should be looking to get ahead of the rest. That's what NZ do, and they keep moving the boundaries and I like that. I coached for many years and got into trouble with refs and the WRU, but the teams I coached won rugby games. When I coached Rumney, a small side on the outskirts of Cardiff, they were in Division 5. Yet we got promoted five consecutive seasons all the way to the Premier Division and didn't even have a grandstand or terracing. I finished after we got to the Premier Division because the challenge was over and there was nowhere else for Rumney to go! There wasn't another division any higher, so what was the point?

I have seen a lot of the new coaches, who have been on all the courses, but have no idea how the game should be played. It is not the problem of the courses, because they are good. It is the people who go on them. They just fancy being a coach. They may be alright to coach kids, and many are not even that good, but you need something else to coach men. I have seen these guys walking out onto the training pitch with more laminated sheets than you can shake a stick at. It takes more than that!

And why do I think Welsh coaches aren't getting to the top? Part of the reason is my answer above. But we did have a Welsh coach before Warren Gatland marched into town. His name was Mike Ruddock, if people can't remember him. When he was in charge, we won the Grand Slam with Wales in 2005, and from where I was sitting he didn't seem to have much support from the WRU. Scott Johnson just looked like he wanted the Welsh job for himself, and some of the senior players stabbed him in the back.

What Mike did, or didn't do, I don't really know. However, Wales won the Grand Slam under him as coach, and in some style as well, I must add. I wonder if Mike had spoken with a New Zealand, an Australian, or perhaps a South African accent, he would he have received a lot more support? Yes, I think he would have! Why didn't the WRU support our own people? Strange, perhaps if we had, or have, a Welsh coach, he, or she, would know too much of the goings on inside the WRU. People from other countries who are employed are not worried about that. It is just a job to them and they can always go back to their own country after their contract finishes.

I have no agenda or favouritism towards Mike Ruddock. In fact I remember trying to stamp on his head at St Helens' in Swansea during one game. I thought his head was on an elastic band because it just kept popping up and down when I eventually did stamp on it, happy days!

## 16. What do you think about the way rugby is today?

There is no comparison between professional as opposed to amateur. I do feel there is less soul in the game today, and I question whether players really love the game enough, or whether they are just treating it as a living. During the amateur days of rugby, we were expected to have a professional attitude and be committed, without being paid a penny. Actually it cost me a lot of money to play rugby at the highest level.

But looking from afar today, I believe we had the best out of the game during my time playing, even if we didn't get money for it. The friendships, the bonds, the camaraderie were special. Today, perhaps some of the ugly rugby players will get better looking girlfriends, no doubt because they are making decent money, walking around all day wearing track suits and driving big cars, and good luck to them.

These guys are big-looking specimens. Many of them often come into the ring way above their natural weight. That doesn't necessarily mean they are fitter, or stronger, just because they work out in a gym all day. From my experience, gym monkeys aren't always physically strong people. Some of the most powerful people you would ever wish to meet never stepped foot in a gym. They spent all day working underground, or cutting down trees. Some of today's players are big, big guys, but have they got the big hearts to go with it?

What I also dislike today is the same-ism. Everyone is doing the same thing. Players are over-coached in a lot of respects, or afraid to do something which hasn't been pre-planned. It's getting very much like American Football, with all the set-plays and patterns. And do we really want that? I hope not!

Every team and player seems to do the same set moves, well, except for New Zealand, who always led from the front. In Wales we just follow like sheep. The game is very stereotyped, very sterile. This isn't good for players and definitely not good for fans.

## 17. Who would be in your all-time best World XV?

1. Charlie Faulkner (Wales)
2. A.N. Other (Wales)
3. Robert Paparemborde  (France)
4. John Eales (Australia)
5. Colin Meads (NZ)
6. Richie McCaw (NZ)
7. Michael Jones (NZ)
8. Buck Shelford (NZ)
9. Terry Holmes (Wales)
10. Phil Bennett (Wales)
11. David Campese (Australia)
12. Danny Gerber (SA)
13. Philippe Sella (France)
14. Gerald Davies (Wales)
15. Serge Blanco (France)
16. Reserve – Back - Jonathan Davies (Wales)
17. Reserve – Forward - Kieran Reed (NZ)

## 18. But if you had to pick the dirtiest and roughest World XV, who would be in your team and why?

1) Keith Murdoch NZ, even if it's just for his infamous punch in the Angel Hotel in Cardiff when he whacked a security guard after wandering down to the kitchens for something to eat in the middle of the night. He got sent home by management as a direct result, but never got home.  He went to Australia and stayed.

2) Spikey Watkins – No need for any reason for his inclusion.

3) Peter Morgan – Boxer and the hardest man in Merthyr.

4) Big Jim Mills – Rugby League player, he would scare Lucifer.

5) John Morgan – Maesteg RFC. Would frighten anyone, ugly bastard.

6) Bryan Gregory – Pontypool RFC. Nicknamed 'fingers' for obvious reasons.

7) Richie McCaw NZ. Tough, dirty, talented and plays to his own rule book.

8) Buck Shelford-NZ. Strong and as hard as nails.

9) Paul Woods –The Beast of Tredegar (RIP)

10) Danny Wilson – For his off-the-field antics and being Ryan Giggs' Dad.

11) Inga Tuigamala – Big and Hard.

12) Sonny Bill Williams – NZ. Boxer and excellent at both League & Union

13) Ray Gravell – Llanelli RFC. Big heart and soul.

14) Jonah Lomu – NZ. Too big not to put in.

15) Roger Gould – Newport RFC. Very tough for a back. Could have played in the pack.

16) Reserve – Forwards - John Perkins – Pontypool RFC. Hard, small & mean.

17) Reserve – Backs - David Bishop – Pontypool RFC. For his off-the-field antics.

## 19. What Players/Coaches impress you today?

– Team – New Zealand: Still way ahead of everyone and they are only a tiny nation.

– Players – Forward: Richie McCaw for his durability.

- Players - Back : George North is a new-breed of back who can do many things
- Coach: Jake White for being successful in both South Africa and Australia.

**20. If you had never played rugby, what other sport would you have liked to have been successful in?**

Boxing or maybe cock-fighting!

**21. Who is your all-time sporting Hero?**

Cassius Clay/ Muhammad Ali. I wouldn't have got up at four in the morning to watch anyone else.

**22. What is your Favourite Film?**

*One Flew Over the Cuckoo's Nest*

**23. What is your Favourite food?**

Tom Yum Goong, a great Thai dish, and anything else Maew cooks me!

**24. Who is your Favourite Band / Singer?**

Barry White. His songs like: *Love Affair*; *Everlasting Love*; *You're the First, My Last, My Everything* are pure class. If I get married to Maew, we'll have to play one of them.

**25. What four people would you invite around for dinner, and why?**

Gordon Ramsay – he can cook and he is such a polite man
George Best – he could choose the drinks
Oliver Reed – he could drink the drinks
Jack Nicholson – for the entertainment

**26. What actor would you have to play Spikey in a Movie?**

John 'Johnny Rotten' Lydon

**27. What would you like to be written on your Gravestone?**

"It was good while it lasted"

# Rugby Career Statistics

| | |
|---|---|
| Crumlin RFC | 198 games - tries (no idea) |
| Cardiff RFC | 129 games - 12 tries |
| Newport RFC | 229 games - 18 tries. 1 conversion |
| Wales | 4 games |
| Wales XV | 1 game (vs. President's World XV to open the old Arms Park) |
| Wales B | 4 games |
| Barbarians | 3 games |
| SA Barbarians | 1 game |
| World XV | 2 games |
| Irish Wolfhounds | 1 game |
| Crawshays | 20+ games |
| Monmouthshire | 20+ games |
| Newbridge | 1 game (sent off) |

# Any Other Business
# The View from the Committee

After marrying a Crumlin girl in 1958, I moved there and consequently in raising a family took a keen interest in most things that took place, particularly rugby football, which practically took over my whole family's lives.

In following the fortunes of Crumlin Rugby Club, I became aware of a very promising young player, their hooker, Mike Watkins, affectionately known as 'Spike'. He had a wicked sense of humour, and even then did not suffer fools gladly. It wasn't long before he attracted the attention of Cardiff Rugby Club and with the best wishes of everyone in Crumlin, he joined Cardiff.

Over the years I noted that Michael played for Wales 'B' against France 'B' in 1976, 1978, 1979 and 1983. He also travelled to Australia with the Welsh Rugby Union Team in 1978. Shortly after this tour, when I refereed a game at Newbridge, Clive Davis of that club, who also toured Australia, informed me that "Spike had trained like a fanatic, impressed everyone, and should have been capped there".

Fast forward now to 1984, when I was a member of the Welsh Rugby Union Committee. To the delight of everyone in Crumlin, Michael J was selected to play for Wales in Ireland, with the added honour of being made captain in his first International,

Traditionally at away Internationals, players gaining their

first cap were presented with them at a private function, which was attended by the whole Committee, Selectors and players of the Welsh Rugby Union Team. As everyone entered the room, Ian Stephens of Bridgend, who had played prop to Michael that afternoon, handed each person a double gin, and prompted each to "down in one". What a start to proceedings! However, there was more to follow, when the time came to present Michael with his cap, the Chairman of Selectors red-facedly explained there was no cap available to present. All eyes switched to the Secretary of The Welsh Rugby Union, a man of few admirers, who had even less at that precise moment. The saving grace was the Welsh Team, that afternoon, had beaten Ireland by 18 points to 9 points, so a good time was had by all, including the capless Michael J.Watkins.

Michael retained his place when we played home to France, which we lost by 16 points to 21 points. So it was on to Twickenham, where Michael's team beat England by 24 points to 15 points. On the Sunday morning we were having breakfast in the Poodle Dog Restaurant of a hotel in Chelsea, when Michael J and John Perkins of Pontypool, walked in, each carrying a pint of Guinness, whilst cracking jokes to the amusement of everyone.

My final memory of Michael J, whilst I was on the Welsh Rugby Union Committee, was in my capacity as Chairman of the Disciplinary Committee, a position I held for 12 years. It was toward the end of his playing career and Michael had transgressed on the field of play, earning the displeasure of the referee, who subsequently sent him off. Michael attended the Disciplinary hearing and explained in terms only he could, how his sending-off transpired. Suffice to say it was hilarious, totally in keeping with a "happy hooker", which in my opinion earned him a lesser sentence!

In bringing to a close my memories of Michael J. Watkins I

am proud to say that knowing him has enriched my life and many others too, in the way he has approached life in general and rugby football, in particular.

**David Rees Johnson, WRU Committeeman**

# The Happy Ending from Bangkok

As an undergraduate at Cardiff University in the early 1980's I used to venture down to Rodney Parade where Mike 'Spikey' Watkins was captain and arguably the finest hooker ever to be produced in Wales. The good oil was that he was a cross between Margaret Thatcher, Ronnie Biggs and the Anti-Christ and not someone to approach. Twenty two years later I was introduced to Spikey at a rugby dinner featuring Jonathan Davies here in Bangkok. Not sure if he had changed or found God but he seemed more of a cross between Mother Theresa, George Best and Peter Pan. A real character always with a good story to tell coupled with a hidden, sharp, brain. I look at him as a good friend and sounding board!

*Gareth Hughes*
*Managing Director*
*RSM Thailand*

# Afterword

My first interview with Spikey took place via Skype on a Sunday afternoon. Nervously I sat in my kitchen in Merthyr, Spikey far away in his home in Bangkok. I thought I'd take the bull by the horns by asking the rugby legend about a story I'd heard about him taking a horse into a swimming pool on a roof of a hotel in South Africa. A story which had become folk law throughout Welsh rugby circles.

Spikey shook his head slowly. 'No...no...no,' he replied.

'I knew it,' I disappointedly thought to myself, just another tall 'cock-and-bull' rugby tale with no truth behind it.

But then he added, 'No, it wasn't a horse. It was a donkey. A horse wouldn't have fitted in the lift.'

A smile cracked my face in two. 'This,' I thought to myself, 'is going to be bloody great ride.' I picked up my pen, opened my note pad and bravely entered the wonderful world of Spikey, and I'm so glad I did.

**Stay free**

**Bunko**

# Index

# INDEX

# INDEX

# INDEX

# INDEX